Stanley Gibbons COLLECT Falkland Islands STAMPS

**WITH
FALKLAND ISLANDS DEPENDENCIES
BRITISH ANTARCTIC TERRITORY
SOUTH GEORGIA AND
SOUTH SANDWICH ISLANDS**

A STANLEY GIBBONS CHECKLIST

2001 Edition

STANLEY GIBBONS LTD
London and Ringwood

*By Appointment to
Her Majesty The Queen,
Stanley Gibbons Ltd., London,
Philatelists*

Published by **Stanley Gibbons Publications**
Editorial, Sales Offices and Distribution Centre:
5 Parkside, Christchurch Road, Ringwood,
Hants BH24 3SH

FIRST EDITION (2001)

ISBN: 0-85259-501-8

© Stanley Gibbons Ltd 2000

Copyright Notice

The contents of this catalogue, including the numbering system and illustrations, are fully protected by copyright. No part of this publication may be reproduced, stored in a retrieval system, or transmitted in any form or by any means, electronic, mechanical, photocopying, recording or otherwise, without the prior permission of Stanley Gibbons Limited. Requests for such permission should be addressed to the Catalogue Editor at Ringwood.
This catalogue is sold on condition that it is not, by way of trade or otherwise, lent, re-sold, hired out, circulated or otherwise disposed of other than in its complete, original and unaltered form and without a similar condition, including this condition, being imposed on the subsequent purchaser.

Item No. 0291 (01)

Text assembled and Printed in Great Britain by
Black Bear Press Limited, Cambridge.

COLLECT FALKLAND ISLANDS STAMPS

Stanley Gibbons have in the past produced several catalogues dedicated to the stamps of the Falkland Islands and other South Atlantic territories. None, however, has been available since the "Two Reigns" volume in 1988, so it is clearly time for the present volume, covering stamps from 1878 to 2000, to appear.

This checklist uses listings extracted from the 2001 edition of the *Part 1 (British Commonwealth) Catalogue* with full colour illustrations taken from the comprehensive picture database being assembled for eventual use in all the Stanley Gibbons catalogues. Stamps from Falkland Islands Dependencies, British Antarctic Territory, and South Georgia and the South Sandwich Islands are also included, with new issues updated to early August 2000.

Layout. Stamps are set out chronologically by date of issue. In the catalogue lists the first numeral is the Stanley Gibbons catalogue number, the black (boldface) numeral alongside is the type number referring to the respective illustration. A blank in this column implies that the number immediately above is repeated. The denomination and colour of the stamp are then shown. Before February 1971 the currency used in the Falkland Islands was:

£1 = 20s One pound = twenty shillings
and
1s = 12d One shilling = twelve pence.
Upon decimalisation this became:
£1 = 100p One pound = one hundred (new) pence.

The catalogue list shows two price columns. The left-hand is for unused stamps and the right-hand for used.

Our method of indicating prices is: Numerals for pence, e.g. 10 denotes 10p (10 pence). Numerals for pounds and pence, e.g. 4·25 (4 pounds and 25 pence). For £100 and above, prices are in whole pounds and so include the £ sign and omit the zeros for pence.

Colour illustrations. The colour illustrations of stamps are intended as a guide only; they may differ in shade from the originals.

Size of illustrations. To comply with Post Office regulations stamp illustrations are three-quarters linear size. Separate illustrations of surcharges, overprints and watermarks are actual size.

Prices. Prices quoted in this catalogue are our selling prices in sterling currency at the time the book went to press. They are for stamps in fine condition; in issues where condition varies we may ask more for the superb and less for the sub-standard. The unused prices for stamps up to 1935 are for lightly hinged examples. Unused prices for issues since 1935 are for unmounted mint (though when not available unmounted, mounted stamps are often supplied at a lower price). Prices for used stamps refer to postally used examples. All prices are subject to change without prior notice and we give no guarantee to supply all stamps priced, since it is not possible to keep every catalogued item in stock. Individual low value stamps sold at 399, Strand are liable to an additional handling charge. Commemorative issues may, at times, only be available in complete sets.

In the price columns:
† = Does not exist.
(—) or blank = Exists, or may exist, but price cannot be quoted.
The minimum catalogue price quoted is 10p. For individual stamps prices between 10p. and 50p. are provided as a guide for catalogue users. The lowest price *charged* for individual stamps purchased from Stanley Gibbons Ltd is 50p.

Set prices are generally for one of each value, excluding shades and varieties, but including major colour changes. Where there are alternative shades, etc., the cheapest is usually included. The number of stamps in the set is always stated for clarity. The mint prices for sets containing *se-tenant* pieces are based on the prices quoted for such combinations and those for used sets on the prices for individual stamps.

Perforations. The "perforation" is the number of holes in a length of 2 cm. as measured by the Gibbons *Instanta* gauge. The stamp is viewed against a dark background with the transparent gauge put on top of it. Perforations are quoted to the nearest half. Stamps without perforation are termed "imperforate".

Watermarks. The following watermark types have been used on the issues of the Falkland Islands:

w **4**
Crown (over) CC

w **6**
Crown (over) CA

w **8**
Multiple Crown CA

w **9**
Multiple Crown Script CA

w **12**
Multiple St. Edward's Crown Block CA

w **14**
Multiple Crown CA Diagonal

w **16**
Multiple Crown Script CA Diagonal

The above illustrations show the watermarks as seen from the *front* of the stamps. This checklist includes varieties showing the watermark inverted, reversed or inverted and reversed.

Specimen Stamps. During the period 1884 to 1928 most of the stamps of British Crown Colonies used for distribution by the Universal Postal Union were overprinted SPECIMEN in various shapes and sizes by their printers from typeset formes. Some locally produced provisionals were hand-stamped locally. From 1928 stamps were punched with holes forming the word SPECIMEN, each firm of printers using a different machine or machines. From 1948 the stamps supplied for U.P.U. distribution were no longer punctured.

Printers and Printing Process. The following abbreviations are used in the checklist to indicate the printer of each issue and the process used:

B.D.T	B.D.T. International Security Printing Ltd, Dublin	P.B.	Perkins Bacon Ltd
B.W.	Bradbury Wilkinson & Co Ltd	Photo	Photogravure
Cartor	Cartor SA, La Loupe	Questa	Questa Colour Security Printers Ltd
Des	Designed	Recess	Recess-printed
D.L.R.	De La Rue & Co Ltd	Walsall	Walsall Security Printers Ltd
Eng	Engraved	Waterlow	Waterlow & Sons Ltd
Enschedé	Joh. Enschedé en Zonen, Haarlem		
Format	Format International Security Printers Ltd		
Harrison	Harrison & Sons Ltd		
J.W.	John Waddington Security Printers Ltd		
Litho	Lithography		

Catalogue numbers used. The checklist uses the same catalogue numbers as the Stanley Gibbons *Part 1 Catalogue*, 2001 Edition.

Latest issue date for stamps recorded in this edition is 4 August 2000.

STANLEY GIBBONS LTD

Head Office: 399 Strand, London WC2R 0LX.

Auction Room and Specialist Stamp Departments. Open Monday–Friday 9.30 a.m. to 5 p.m.
Shop. Open Monday to Friday 8.30 a.m. to 6 p.m. and Saturday 9.30 a.m. to 5.30 p.m.

Telephone: 020 7836 8444 for all departments.
E-mail: enquiries@stanleygibbons.co.uk
Website: www.stanleygibbons.com

Stanley Gibbons Publications:
5 Parkside, Christchurch Road,
Ringwood, Hants BH24 3SH
Telephone: 01425 472363
Publications Mail Order
FREEPHONE: 0800 611622
E-mail: info@stanleygibbons.co.uk

FALKLAND ISLANDS PHILATELIC BUREAU

new issues

All Falkland Islands' new issues are available directly from the Philatelic Bureau and from Sovereign Stamps, the Crown Agents Stamp Bureau retail operation:-

Falkland Islands Philatelic Bureau
Stanley
Falkland Islands
E-mail: philatelic.fig@horizon.co.fk
Web site: www.falklands.gov.fk/pb/home.htm

Sovereign Stamps, P O Box 123, Sutton,
Surrey, SM1 4WH, UK.
Tel: 020 8770 1373
E-mail: casb@compuserve.com
Web site: www.casb.co.uk

Stanley Gibbons
Mail Order Department Presents ...

Quality Stamps Delivered Direct to Your Door

Irresistibly simple, exceptionally quick and reassuringly reliable, Stanley Gibbons philatelic Mail Order Service enables you to economically build your collection from the comfort of your own surroundings.

Free 2000 Falkland Islands Listing

- A complete listing of our current Falkland Islands stock.
- Packed full of popular material, complete with a selection of illustrations and accurate descriptions.
- Contains a useful checklist and a pull out order form in the centre pages.
- Many rare and specialised items are now included.
- Makes collecting easy, from the comfort of your own home.

Other FREE mail order commonwealth stamp lists include:

Australia and States	Channel Islands & Isle of Man
British Europe	Collector's Bookshelf
British Far East	Great Britain
British West Indies	Indian States
Canada	New Zealand

To send for your FREE copy of the Falkland Islands listing or any other Mail Order stamp brochure please phone our Mail Order Department FREE on 0800 731 8052 (UK only). Alternatively contact Mark Leonard at our London office.

Stanley Gibbons Mail Order
399 Strand, London, WC2R 0LX, United Kingdom.
Tel: +44 (0)20 7836 8444 Fax: +44 (0)20 7836 7342
email: mailorder@stanleygibbons.co.uk
Internet: www.stanleygibbons.com

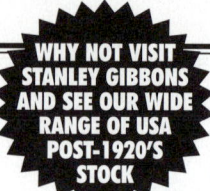
WHY NOT VISIT STANLEY GIBBONS AND SEE OUR WIDE RANGE OF USA POST-1920'S STOCK

BY APPOINTMENT TO HER MAJESTY THE QUEEN STANLEY GIBBONS LTD LONDON, PHILATELISTS

Stanley Gibbons
The World's Oldest and Most Famous Name in Stamps

THE COMPLETE COLLECTORS SERVICE FROM A SINGLE SOURCE

With millions of stamps in stock at any time, we cater for the requirements of ALL collectors - from the eager beginner to the ardent connoisseur.

Whether you are seeking an elusive piece of postal history, a valuation, varieties and errors, thematics, philatelic books, a comprehensive range of stamp catalogues, albums and accessories, or perhaps a different collectables gift - all are to be found in our exciting and well stocked shop in The Strand, London.

Stanley Gibbons - serving customers in The Strand for over 135 years

STANLEY GIBBONS SHOP, 399 THE STRAND, LONDON WC2R 0LX, UNITED KINGDOM
Leading Philatelists since 1856

Tel: +44 (0) 20-7836-8444 Fax: +44 (0) 20-7836-7342
email: shop@stanleygibbons.co.uk   internet: www.stanleygibbons.com

Shop opening hours:
Monday - Friday 8.30 am - 6.00 pm   Saturday 9.30 am - 5.30 pm
Sunday 10.00 am - 4.00 pm

(very close to Adelphi and Vaudeville Theatres,
6 mins from Charing Cross Station)

LEAVE YOUR COLLECTION IN RELIABLE HANDS

For Collectors who want their Collection to Look its Best

Stanley Gibbons and Davo Standard and Luxury Hingeless Albums

Stanley Gibbons and Davo albums are highly elegant yet robust. The extra-heavy board binders are attractively covered in uniform navy blue, emblazoned on both the cover and spine with the crest of the Falkland Islands. Solid brass screw peg-fittings hold the acid-free album leaves firmly in place, whilst allowing for the easy removal and rearrangement of pages and the addition of new supplements published each year. If you want your collection to look its best, then look no further.

Item No. 5451 Falkland Islands Volume 1 (1878-1995) £89.95
Item No. 5452 Falkland Islands Volume 3 (1996-1999) £49.95
Item No. 5455 Falkland Dependencies (1944-1999) £69.95
Item No. 5458 British Antarctic Territory (1963-1999) pages only £44.95
Item No. 5451(SO) Falkland Islands Set Offer SAVE £29+ £224.95

To order or for further information, please phone our Customer Services Department for **FREE** on **0800 611 622** (UK only) quoting reference FALK/00. Alternatively, order online
www.stanleygibbons.com

STANLEY GIBBONS PUBLICATIONS
5 Parkside, Christchurch Road, Ringwood,
Hants, BH24 3SH, United Kingdom.
Tel: +44 (0)1425 472363   Fax: +44 (0)1425 470247
email: sales@stanleygibbons.co.uk

ROBIN MURCHIE

Specialising in the Stamps, Postal History, Postcards and Ephemera of:-

The Falkland Islands and Antarctica,
Ascension, St Helena, and Tristan Da Cunha.

Regular auction catalogues and price lists. Wants lists welcomed.

Collections and better single items from these areas always required.

PENN COTTAGE, EAST MARTIN, FORDINGBRIDGE, SP6 3LJ, UK
Telephone/Fax: 01725 519386

The **exciting new** online community for stamp collectors...

where enthusiasts can receive information on new issues and advice about the hobby of stamp collecting.

You can contact us at the following email address for further information...
info@stampcafe.com

stampcafe sponsored by

www.stampcafe.com

Falkland Islands

1878 12 pence (d) = 1 shilling
20 shillings = 1 pound
1971 100 (new) pence = 1 pound

PRICES FOR STAMPS ON COVER TO 1945	
No. 1	from × 70
No. 2	from × 50
Nos. 3/4	from × 10
No. 5	—
Nos. 6/10	from × 30
Nos. 11/12	from × 15
Nos. 13/17	from × 10
Nos. 17b/c	from × 100
Nos. 18/21	from × 10
Nos. 22/b	from × 30
Nos. 23/4	from × 100
Nos. 25/6	from × 30
No. 27	from × 20
No. 28	from × 40
No. 29	from × 5
Nos. 30/b	from × 50
No. 30c	from × 15
No. 31	from × 5
Nos. 32/8	from × 15
Nos. 41/2	—
Nos. 43/8	from × 12
Nos. 49/50	—
Nos. 60/5	from × 10
Nos. 66/9	—
Nos. 70/1	from × 10
Nos. 72/b	—
Nos. 73/9	from × 4
No. 80	—
No. 115	from × 2
Nos. 116/19	from × 20
Nos. 120/2	from × 6
Nos. 123/6	—
Nos. 127/34	from × 5
Nos. 135/8	—
Nos. 139/45	from × 50
Nos. 146/63	from × 5

CROWN COLONY

1

2

1869–76. *The Franks.*
FR1 1 In black, *on cover* £6500
FR2 2 In red, *on cover* (1876) £12000
On *piece*, No. FR1 on white or coloured paper £90; No. FR2 on white £130. The use of these franks ceased when the first stamps were issued.
The first recorded use of No. FR1 is on a cover to London datestamped 4 January 1869.

3   (4)

In the ½d., 2d., 2½d. and 9d. the figures of value in the lower corners are replaced by small rosettes and the words of value are in colour.

NOTE. Nos. 1, 2, 3, 4, 8, 10, 11 and 12 exist with one or two sides imperf from the margin of the sheets.

(Recess B.W.)

1878–79. *No wmk. P* 14, 14½.
1 3 1d. claret (19.6.78) £550 £325
2   4d. grey-black (Sept 1879) .. £1000 £150
      a. On wmkd paper £2500 £500
3   6d. blue-green (19.6.78) .. 55·00 50·00
4   1s. bistre-brown (1878) .. 50·00 50·00
No. 2a shows portions of the papermaker's watermark—"R. TURNER, CHAFFORD MILLS"—in ornate double-lined capitals.

NOTES. The dates shown for Nos. 5/12 and 15/38 are those on which the printer delivered the various printings to the Crown Agents. Several months could elapse before the stamps went on sale in the Colony, depending on the availability of shipping

The plates used for these stamps did not fit the paper so that the watermark appears in all sorts of positions on the stamp. Well centred examples are scarce. Examples can also be found showing parts of the marginal watermarks, either CROWN AGENTS horizontally in letters 12 mm high or "CROWN AGENTS FOR THE COLONIES" vertically in 7 mm letters. Both are in double-lined capitals.

1882 (22 Nov). *Wmk Crown CA* (*upright*). *P* 14, 14½.
5 3 1d. dull claret £325 £120
      a. Imperf vert (horiz pair) .. £42000
      y. Wmk inverted and reversed £400 £225
6   4d. grey-black .. .. .. £250 70·00
      w. Wmk inverted £400 £160

1885 (23 Mar)–**87.** *Wmk Crown CA* (*sideways**). *P* 14, 14½.
7 3 1d. pale claret .. .. .. 55·00 38·00
      w. Wmk Crown to right of CA .. 75·00 50·00
      x. Wmk sideways reversed .. £150 90·00
      y. Wmk Crown to right of CA and reversed .. .. .. £150 90·00
8   1d. brownish claret (3.10.87) .. 80·00 38·00
      a. Bisected (on cover) (1891) † .. †£2000
      w. Wmk Crown to right of CA .. 90·00 42·00
      x. Wmk sideways reversed .. £120 £100
      y. Wmk Crown to right of CA and reversed £150 £120
9   4d. pale grey-black .. .. £425 42·00
      w. Wmk Crown to right of CA .. £450 50·00
      x. Wmk sideways reversed .. £550 £150
      y. Wmk Crown to right of CA and reversed £550 £100
10   4d. grey-black (3.10.87) .. £325 35·00
      w. Wmk Crown to right of CA .. £325 35·00
      x. Wmk sideways reversed .. £550 90·00
      y. Wmk Crown to right of CA and reversed .. .. .. £450 60·00

*The normal sideways watermark shows Crown to left of CA, as seen from the back of the stamp.
†See note below No. 14.

2 — Falkland Islands   1889

1889 (26 Sept)–**91**. *Wmk Crown CA (upright). P* 14, 14½.
11	3	1d. red-brown (21.5.91)		.. £140	65·00
		a. Bisected (on cover)*			†£2250
		x. Wmk reversed		.. £300	£160
12		4d. olive grey-black		.. £110	45·00
		w. Wmk inverted		.. £350	£225
		x. Wmk reversed		.. £275	£110

See note below No. 14.

1891 (Jan). *Nos. 8 and 11 bisected diagonally and each half handstamped with T* **4**.
13	3	½d. on half of 1d. brownish claret (No. 8)		£500	£300
		a. Unsevered pair		£2250	£1000
		b. Unsevered pair *se-tenant* with unsurcharged whole stamp			.. £13000
		c. Bisect *se-tenant* with unsurcharged whole stamp			†£1200
14		½d. on half 1d. red-brown (No. 11)		.. £550	£250
		a. Unsevered pair		£2500	£1200
		b. Bisect *se-tenant* with unsurcharged whole stamp			†£1100

1891 PROVISIONALS. In 1891 the postage to the United Kingdom and Colonies was reduced from 4d. to 2½d. per half ounce. As no ½d. or 2½d. stamps were available the bisection of the 1d. was authorised from 1 January 1891. This authorisation was withdrawn on 11 January 1892, although bisects were accepted for postage until July of that year. The ½d. and 2½d. stamps were placed on sale from 10 September 1891.

Cork Cancel used in 1891

The Type **4** surcharge was not used regularly; unsurcharged bisects being employed far more frequently. Genuine bisects should be cancelled with the cork cancel illustrated above. The use of any other postmark, including a different cork cancel, requires date evidence linked to known mail ship sailings to prove authenticity.

Posthumous strikes of the surcharge on "souvenir" bisects usually show a broken "2" and/or a large full stop. These are known on bisected examples of No. 18 and on varieties such as surcharge inverted, double or sideways. Forgeries exist of all these provisionals.

1891 (10 Sept*)–**1902**. *Wmk Crown CA (upright). P* 14, 14½.
15	3	½d. blue-green (Aug–Nov 1891)		20·00	26·00
		x. Wmk reversed		.. £225	£225
		y. Wmk inverted and reversed		.. £225	£225
16		½d. green (20.5.92)		.. 16·00	15·00
		ax. Wmk reversed		.. £110	£110
		ay. Wmk inverted and reversed		.. £225	£225
		b. *Deep dull green* (15.4.96)		.. 40·00	30·00
17		½d. deep yellow-green (1894–95)		.. 17·00	21·00
		ay. Wmk inverted and reversed		.. £110	£110
		b. *Yellow-green* (19.6.99)		.. 2·00	2·50
		c. *Dull yellowish green* (13.1.1902)		.. 5·00	4·00
		cx. Wmk reversed		.. £225	£225
18		1d. orange red-brown (14.10.91)		.. 60·00	48·00
		a. *Brown*		.. 80·00	50·00
		w. Wmk inverted		.. £550	£275
		x. Wmk reversed		.. £150	£150
19		1d. reddish chestnut (20.4.92)		.. 40·00	42·00
20		1d. orange-brn (wmk reversed) (18.1.94)		42·00	42·00
21		1d. claret (23.7.94)		.. 80·00	80·00
		x. Wmk reversed		.. 55·00	50·00
22		1d. Venetian red (pale to deep) (1895–96)		15·00	14·00
		ax. Wmk reversed		.. 9·00	10·00
		b. *Venetian claret* (1898?)		.. 28·00	12·00
23		1d. pale red (19.6.99)		.. 5·00	2·00
		x. Wmk reversed		.. £160	£160
24		1d. orange-red (13.1.1902)		.. 9·00	4·00
25		2d. purple (pale to deep) (1895–98)		.. 6·50	12·00
		x. Wmk reversed		.. £250	£275
26		2d. reddish purple (15.4.96)		.. 5·00	11·00
27		2½d. pale chalky ultramarine (8.91)		.. £120	38·00
28	3	2½d. dull blue (19.11.91)		.. £110	18·00
		x. Wmk reversed		.. £250	£225
29		2½d. Prussian blue (18.1.94)		.. £225	£130
30		2½d. ultramarine (1894–96)		.. 20·00	9·00
		ax. Wmk reversed		.. 35·00	10·00
		b. *Pale ultramarine* (10.6.98)		.. 26·00	13·00
		bx. Wmk reversed		.. £100	75·00
		c. *Deep ultramarine* (18.9.1901)		.. 30·00	30·00
		cx. Wmk reversed		.. £190	£190
31		4d. brownish black (wmk reversed) (18.1.94)			£600 £275
32		4d. olive-black (11.5.95)		.. 10·00	21·00
33		6d. orange-yellow (19.11.91)		.. £150	£130
		x. Wmk reversed		.. 45·00	38·00
34		6d. yellow (15.4.96)		.. 27·00	35·00
35		9d. pale reddish orange (15.11.95)		.. 30·00	55·00
		x. Wmk reversed		.. £200	£225
		y. Wmk inverted and reversed		.. £300	£300
36		9d. salmon (15.4.96)		.. 35·00	48·00
		x. Wmk reversed		.. £200	£225
37		1s. grey-brown (15.11.95)		.. 42·00	45·00
		x. Wmk reversed		.. £120	£120
38		1s. yellow-brown (15.4.96)		.. 40·00	40·00
		w. Wmk reversed		.. £120	£120
15/38			Set of 8	£120	£150
15, 26, 28, 33, 35 Optd "Specimen"			Set of 5	£600	

*The ½d. and 2½d. were first placed on sale in the Falkland Islands on 10 September 1891. Such stamps came from the August 1891 printing. It is now believed that the stock of the May printings sent to the Falkland Islands was lost at sea.

The 2½d. ultramarine printing can sometimes be found in a violet shade, but the reason for this is unknown.

5   6

(Recess B.W.)

1898 (5 Oct). *Wmk Crown CC. P* 14, 14½.
41	5	2s. 6d. deep blue		.. £200	£250
42	6	5s. red		.. £170	£200
41/2 Optd "Specimen"			Set of 2	£450	

7   8

(Recess D.L.R.)

1904 (16 July)–**12**. *Wmk Mult Crown CA. P* 14.
43	7	½d. yellow-green		4·25	1·50
		aw. Wmk inverted		.. £170	£120
		b. *Pale yell-grn* (on thick paper) (6.08)	13·00	9·00
		bw. Wmk inverted			
		c. *Deep yellow-green* (7.11)		.. 9·00	3·00
44		1d. vermilion		.. 9·50	1·50
		aw. Wmk inverted		.. £170	£130
		ax. Wmk reversed		.. £250	£225
		b. *Wmk sideways* (7.06)		.. 1·00	2·50
		c. *Thick paper* (1908)		.. 13·00	1·75
		cw. Wmk inverted		.. £275	£225
		cx. Wmk reversed		.. £350	£225
		d. *Dull coppery red* (on thick paper) (3.08)		.. £170	35·00
		dx. Wmk reversed		.. £500	£225
		e. *Orange-vermilion* (7.11)		.. 11·00	2·50
		ex. Wmk reversed		.. £275	£275

1904 Falkland Islands — 3

45	7		2d. purple (27.12.04)	.. ..	13·00	26·00
		ax.	Wmk reversed	.. .. £110	£110
		b.	Reddish purple (13.1.12)	.. £225	£275
46			2½d. ultramarine (shades)	.. 29·00	7·50
		aw.	Wmk inverted	.. £150	£140
		ay.	Wmk inverted and reversed	—	£375
		b.	Deep blue (13.1.12) ..	.. £225	£180
47			6d. orange (27.12.04)	.. 38·00	48·00
48			1s. brown (27.12.04)	.. 40·00	32·00
49	8		3s. green	.. £140	£130
		aw.	Wmk inverted	.. £1000	
		b.	Deep green (4.07)	.. £120	£120
		bx.	Wmk reversed	.. £1000	£700
50			5s. red (27.12.04)	.. £150	£150
43/50				Set of 8 £350	£350
43/50 Optd "Specimen"				Set of 8 £475	

Examples of Nos. 41/50 and earlier issues are known with a forged Falkland Islands postmark dated "OCT 15 10".

> For details of South Georgia underprint, South Georgia provisional handstamps and Port Foster handstamp see under FALKLAND ISLANDS DEPENDENCIES.

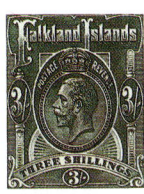

9 **10**

Des B. MacKennal. Eng J. A. C. Harrison. Recess D.L.R.)

1912 (3 July)–**20.** *Wmk Mult Crown CA. P* 13¾×14 *(comb)* (½d. to 1s.) *or* 14 *(line)* (3s. to £1).

60	9		½d. yellow-green	2·75	3·50
		a.	Perf 14 (line). Dp yell-green (1914)	18·00	35·00
		b.	Perf 14 (line). Deep olive (1918)	24·00	85·00
		c.	Deep olive (4.19)	3·50	25·00
		ca.	Printed both sides ..	†	£5500
		d.	Dull yellowish green (on thick greyish paper) (1920)	4·50	27·00
61			1d. orange-red ..	5·50	2·50
		a.	Perf 14 (line). Orange-vermilion (1914, 1916)	23·00	2·50
		b.	Perf 14 (line). Vermilion (1918)	†	£600
		c.	Orange-vermilion (4.19)	3·50	3·00
		d.	Orange-vermilion (on thick greyish paper) (1920)	7·00	2·00
		dx.	Wmk reversed	£140	
62			2d. maroon	23·00	23·00
		a.	Perf 14 (line). Dp reddish pur (1914)	85·00	80·00
		b.	Perf 14 (line). Maroon (4.18)	85·00	80·00
		c.	Deep reddish purple (4.19)	7·00	16·00
63			2½d. deep bright blue	19·00	23·00
		a.	Perf 14 (line). Dp bright blue (1914)	27·00	29·00
		b.	Perf 14 (line). Deep blue (1916, 4.18)	27·00	29·00
		c.	Deep blue (4.19)	7·00	17·00
64			6d. yellow-orange (6.7.12)	14·00	20·00
		aw.	Wmk inverted	£300	£325
		b.	Brown-orange (4.19)	12·00	38·00
65			1s. light bistre-brown (6.7.12) ..	30·00	30·00
		a.	Pale bistre-brown (4.19)	48·00	85·00
		b.	Brn (on thick greyish paper) (1920)	32·00	£130
66	10		3s. slate-green ..	75·00	80·00
67			5s. deep rose-red	75·00	95·00
		a.	Reddish maroon (1914)	£180	£200
		b.	Maroon (1916)	75·00	£100
		bx.	Wmk reversed	£1900	£1200
68			10s. red/green (11.2.14) ..	£150	£250
69			£1 black/red (11.2.14) ..	£350	£400
60/9 (inc 67b)				Set of 11 £700	£900
60/9 (inc 67a) Optd "Specimen" ..				Set of 11 £1300	

The exact measurement of the comb perforation used for Type **9** is 13.7×13.9. The line perforation, used for the 1914, 1916 and 1918 printings and for all the high values in Type **10**, measured 14.1×14.1.

It was previously believed that all examples of the 1d. in vermilion with the line perforation were overprinted to form No. 71, but it has now been established that some unoverprinted sheets of No. 61b were used during 1919.

Many of the sheets showed sheets from the left-hand side in a lighter shade than those from the right. It is believed that this was due to the weight of the impression. Such differences are particularly noticeable on the 2½d. 1916 and 1918 printings where the lighter shades, approaching milky blue in appearance, are scarce.

All 1919 printings show weak impressions of the background either side of the head caused by the poor paper quality.

Examples of all values are known with forged postmarks, including one of Falkland Islands dated "5 SP 19" and another of South Shetlands dated "20 MR 27".

WAR STAMP
(11)

2½D
(12)

1918 (22 Oct*)–**20.** *Optd by Govt Printing Press, Stanley, with T* 11.

70	9		½d. deep olive (line perf) (No. 60b)	.. 1·00	7·00
		a.	Yellow-green (No. 60) (4.19)	.. 14·00	
		ab.	Albino opt ..	.. £1100	
		b.	Deep olive (comb perf) (No. 60c) (4.19	50	6·50
		c.	Dull yellowish green (on thick greyish paper) (No. 60d) (5.20)	.. 12·00	65·00
		cx.	Wmk reversed	£160	
71			1d. vermilion (line perf) (No. 61b)	.. 2·00	18·00
		a.	Opt double, one albino	£400	
		b.	Orge-verm (line perf) (No. 61a) (4.19)	13·00	†
		c.	Orge-verm (comb perf) (No. 61c) (4.19)	50	3·50
		ca.	Opt double ..	.. £1600	
		cx.	Wmk reversed	£275	
		d.	Orange-vermilion (on thick greyish paper) (No. 61d) (5.20)	.. 75·00	£150
72			1s. light bistre-brown (No. 65) ..	30·00	70·00
		a.	Pale bistre-brown (No. 65a) (4.19)	4·00	42·00
		ab.	Opt double, one albino	.. £1200	
		ac.	Opt omitted (in pair with normal) ..	£6000	
		b.	Brown (on thick greyish paper) (No 65b) (5.20) ..	7·00	42·00
		ba.	Opt double, one albino	.. £1200	
		bw.	Wmk inverted	£160	£225
		bx.	Wmk reversed	£500	

*Earliest known postal use. Cancellations dated 8 October were applied much later.

There were five printings of the "WAR STAMP" overprint, but all, except that in May 1920, used the same setting. Composition of the five printings was as follows:

October 1918. Nos. 70, 71 and 72
January 1919. Nos. 70, 71 and 72
April 1919. Nos. 70/b, 71b/c and 72a
October 1919. Nos. 70b, 71c and 72a
May 1920. Nos. 70c, 71d and 72.

It is believed that the entire stock of No. 70a was sold to stamp dealers. Only a handful of used examples are known which may have subsequently been returned to the colony for cancellation.

No. 71ca exists in a block of 12 (6×2) from the bottom of a sheet on which the first stamp in the bottom row shows a single overprint, but the remainder have overprint double.

Examples of Nos. 70/2 are known with a forged Falkland Islands postmark dated "5 SP 19".

1921–28. *Wmk Mult Script CA. P* 14.

73	9		½d. yellowish green	.. 3·00	4·00
		a.	Green (1925)	.. 3·00	4·00
74			1d. dull vermilion (1924)	.. 5·00	1·25
		aw.	Wmk inverted	.. —	†£1100
		ay.	Wmk inverted and reversed	£200	
		b.	Orange-vermilion (shades) (1925)	.. 5·50	1·25
75			2d. deep brown-purple (8.23)	.. 12·00	7·00
		aw.	Wmk inverted	.. —	£950
		ax.	Wmk reversed	.. £1000	
		b.	Purple-brown (1927)	.. 14·00	17·00
		c.	Reddish maroon (1.28)	.. 8·00	20·00
		cy.	Wmk inverted and reversed		
76			2½d. deep blue	.. 22·00	16·00
		a.	Indigo (28.4.27)	.. 16·00	20·00
		b.	Deep steel-blue (1.28)	.. 6·00	16·00
		c.	Prussian blue (10.28)	.. £300	£450

4 — Falkland Islands 1921

77	**9**	2½d. deep purple/*pale yellow* (8.23)	..	4·50	32·00
		a. *Pale purple/pale yellow* (1925)	..	4·25	32·00
		y. Wmk inverted and reversed	..	£250	
78		6d. yellow-orange (1925)	..	8·00	38·00
		w. Wmk inverted	..	£170	
		x. Wmk reversed	..	£900	
79		1s. deep ochre	..	16·00	48·00
80	**10**	3s. slate-green (8.23)	..	80·00	£140
73/80		..	Set of 8	£120	£250
73/80 (*incl* 76a) Optd "Specimen"			Set of 9	£600	

Dates quoted above are those of despatch from Great Britain. No. 76c only occurred in part of the October 1928 printing. The remainder were in the deep steel-blue shade of the January 1928 despatch, No. 76b.

1928 (7 Feb). *No. 75b surch with T* **12**.

115	**9**	2½d. on 2d. purple-brown	..	£700	£750
		a. Surch double		£30000	

No. 115 was produced on South Georgia during a shortage of 2½d. stamps. The provisional was withdrawn on 22 February 1928.

13 Fin Whale and Gentoo Penguins 14

(Recess P.B.)

1929 (2 Sept)–**36**. *P* 14 (*comb*). (*a*) *Wmk Mult Script CA*.

116	**13**	½d. green	..	90	3·00
		a. Line perf (1936)	..	4·00	8·00
117		1d. scarlet	..	3·25	80
		a. Line perf. *Deep red* (1936)	..	6·50	14·00
118		2d. grey	..	2·50	2·00
119		2½d. blue	..	2·75	2·25
120	**14**	4d. orange (*line perf*) (18.2.32)	..	14·00	13·00
		a. *Deep orange* (1936)		32·00	48·00
121	**13**	6d. purple	..	15·00	13·00
		a. Line perf. *Reddish purple* (1936)		38·00	27·00
122		1s. black/*emerald*	..	18·00	30·00
		a. Line perf. *On bright emerald* (1936)	23·00	27·00
123		2s. 6d carmine/*blue*	..	38·00	45·00
124		5s. green/*yellow*	..	60·00	80·00
125		10s. carmine/*emerald*	..	£110	£150

(*b*) *Wmk Mult Crown CA*

126	**13**	£1 black/*red*	..	£275	£375
116/26			Set of 11	£475	£650
116/26 Perf "Specimen"			Set of 11	£1000	

Two kinds of perforation exist:
A. Comb perf 13.9:—original values of 1929.
B. Line perf 13.9×14.2 or 14.2 (small holes)—4d. and 1936 printings of ½d., 1d., 6d. and 1s. On some sheets the last vertical row of perforations shows larger holes.

Examples of most values are known with forged postmarks, including one of Port Stanley dated "14 JY 31" and another of South Georgia dated "AU 30 31".

15 Romney Marsh Ram   26 King George V

(Des (except 6d.) by G. Roberts. Eng and recess B.W.)

1933 (2 Jan–Apr). *Centenary of British Administration. T* **15**, **26** *and similar designs. Wmk Mult Script CA. P* 12.

127	½d. black and green	..	1·50	5·00
128	1d. black and scarlet	..	3·50	2·25
129	1½d. black and blue	..	10·00	13·00
130	2d. black and brown	..	9·00	22·00
131	3d. black and violet	..	11·00	14·00
132	4d. black and orange	..	13·00	15·00
133	6d. black and slate	..	50·00	60·00
134	1s. black and olive-green		40·00	55·00
135	2s. 6d. black and violet	..	£140	£170
136	5s. black and yellow	..	£500	£650
	a. *Black and yellow-orange* (Apr)		£1100	£1300
137	10s. black and chestnut		£500	£750
138	£1 black and carmine	..	£1400	£1900
127/138	..	Set of 12	£2250	£3250
127/38 Perf "Specimen"		Set of 12	£2250	

Designs: *Horiz*—1d. Iceberg; 1½d. Whale-catcher *Bransfield*; 2d. Port Louis; 3d. Map of Falkland Islands; 4d. South Georgia; 6d. Fin Whale; 1s. Government House, Stanley. *Vert*—2s. 6d. Battle Memorial; 5s. King Penguin; 10s. Coat of Arms.

Examples of all values are known with forged Port Stanley postmarks dated "6 JA 33". Some values have also been seen with part strikes of the forged Falkland Islands postmark mentioned below Nos. 60/9 and 70/2.

26a Windsor Castle

Extra flagstaff (Plate "1" R. 9/1)   Short extra flagstaff (Plate "2" R. 2/1)

Lightning conductor (Plate "3" R. 2/5)   Flagstaff on right-hand turret (Plate "5" R. 7/1)

Double flagstaff (Plate "6" R. 5/2)

1935 Falkland Islands — 5

(Des H. Fleury. Recess B.W.)

1935 (7 May). *Silver Jubilee. Wmk Mult Script CA.* P 11×12.
139	26a	1d. deep blue and scarlet	..	3·50	40
		b. Short extra flagstaff	..	£325	£200
		d. Flagstaff on right-hand turret		£200	£150
		e. Double flagstaff ..	..	£250	£180
140		2½d. brown and deep blue	..	9·00	1·75
		b. Short extra flagstaff	..	£750	£400
		d. Flagstaff on right-hand turret		£225	£160
		e. Double flagstaff ..	..	£350	£200
		l. Re-entry on value tablet (R. 8/1)		£200	£100
141		4d. green and indigo	..	11·00	4·50
		b. Short extra flagstaff	..	£500	£325
		d. Flagstaff on right-hand turret		£325	£200
		e. Double flagstaff ..	..	£375	£250
142		1s. slate and purple ..	..	8·00	3·50
		a. Extra flagstaff	..	£2750	£2250
		b. Short extra flagstaff	..	£550	£300
		c. Lightning conductor	..	£1000	£700
		d. Flagstaff on right-hand turret		£500	£325
		e. Double flagstaff ..	..	£550	£350
139/42		.. .. ..	Set of 4	28·00	9·00
139/42 Perf "Specimen"	.. ..	Set of 4	£300		

26b King George VI and Queen Elizabeth

(Des D.L.R. Recess B.W.)

1937 (12 May). *Coronation. Wmk Mult Script CA.* P 11×11½.
143	26b	½d. green	..	30	10
144		1d. carmine ..	..	40	45
145		2½d. blue	..	80	80
143/5		.. .. ..	Set of 3	1·40	1·25
143/5 Perf "Specimen"	.. ..	Set of 3	£160		

27 Whales' Jaw Bones

(Des G. Roberts (Nos. 146, 148/9, 158 and 160/3), K. Lellman (No. 159). Recess B.W.)

1938 (3 Jan)–**50**. *Horiz designs as T 27. Wmk Mult Script CA.* P 12.
146		½d. black and green (*shades*)	..	30	75
147		1d. black and carmine	..	27·00	80
		a. Black and scarlet..	..	3·75	85
148		1d. black and violet (14.7.41)	..	2·50	1·75
		a. Black and purple-violet (1.43)		7·00	75
149		2d. black and deep violet	..	1·00	50
150		2d. black and carmine-red (14.7.41)..		75	2·25
		a. Black and red (1.43)	..	2·75	1·00
151		2d. black and bright blue	..	1·25	30
152		2½d. black and blue (15.6.49) ..		6·50	7·00
153		3d. black and blue (14.7.41) ..		6·50	2·50
		a. Black and deep blue (1.43)	..	9·00	2·50
154		4d. black and purple ..	..	2·75	50
155		6d. black and brown ..	..	3·25	1·50
156		6d. black (15.6.49) ..	..	5·00	3·75
157		9d. black and grey-blue	..	13·00	90
158		1s. pale blue ..	..	65·00	18·00
		a. Deep blue (1941)	..	16·00	2·50
159		1s. 3d. black and carmine-red (11.12.46)		2·50	1·40
160		2s. 6d. slate ..	..	55·00	10·00
161		5s. bright blue and pale brown	..	£110	60·00
		b. Indigo and yellow-brown (1942)		£600	£100
		c. Blue and buff-brown (9.2.50)	..	£140	£170
162		10s. black and orange	..	55·00	27·00
163		£1 black and violet	..	£110	48·00
146/63		.. .. ..	Set of 18	£350	£140
146/63 (*ex* 152, 156) Perf "Specimen"	Set of 16	£950			

Designs:—Nos. 147 and 150, Black-necked Swan; Nos. 148/9, Battle Memorial; Nos. 151 and 153, Flock of sheep; Nos. 152 and 154, Magellan Goose; Nos. 155/6, *Discovery II* (polar supply vessel); No. 157, *William Scoresby* (research ship); No. 158, Mount Sugar Top; No. 159; Turkey Vultures; No. 160 Gentoo Penguins; No. 161, Southern Sealion; No. 162, Deception Island; No. 163, Arms of Falkland Islands.

28 Houses of Parliament, London

(Des and recess D.L.R.)

1946 (7 Oct). *Victory. Wmk Mult Script CA.* P 13½×14.
164	28	1d. dull violet ..	..	30	15
165		3d. blue	..	45	15
164/5 Perf "Specimen"	.. ..	Set of 2	£140		

29 30
King George VI and Queen Elizabeth

(Des and photo Waterlow (T **29**). Design recess, name typo B.W. (T **30**))

1948 (1 Nov). *Royal Silver Wedding. Wmk Mult Script CA.*
166	29	2½d. ultramarine (p 14×15) ..	..	2·00	85
167	30	£1 mauve (p 11½×11)	..	90·00	55·00

31 Hermes, Globe and Forms of Transport

32 Hemispheres, Jet-powered Vickers Viking Airliner and Steamer

33 Hermes, Globe and Envelopes

34 U.P.U. Monument

6 — Falkland Islands 1949

(Recess Waterlow (T **31, 34**). Designs recess, name typo B.W. (T **32/3**))

1949 (10 Oct). *75th Anniv of Universal Postal Union. Wmk Mult Script CA.*
168	**31**	1d. violet (p 13½–14)	..	..	1·50	75
169	**32**	3d. deep blue (p 11×11½)	..	..	5·00	2·00
170	**33**	1s. 3d. deep blue-green (p 11×11½)		..	4·00	2·25
171	**34**	2s. blue (p 13½–14)	..	..	4·00	7·50
168/71		..	..	Set of 4	13·00	11·00

39 Sheep

43 Arms of the Colony

(Des from sketches by V. Spencer. Recess Waterlow)

1952 (2 Jan). *T* **39, 43** *and similar designs. Wmk Mult Script CA. P* 13×13½ *(vert) or* 13½×13 *(horiz).*
172	½d. green		..	70	70
173	1d. scarlet	..	..	1·50	40
174	2d. violet	..	..	3·50	2·50
175	2½d. black and light ultramarine		..	95	50
176	3d. deep ultramarine	..	..	1·00	1·00
177	4d. reddish purple	..	..	7·50	1·50
178	6d. bistre-brown	..	..	12·00	1·00
179	9d. orange-yellow	..	..	9·00	2·00
180	1s. black	..	..	22·00	80
181	1s. 3d. orange	..	..	13·00	5·00
182	2s. 6d. olive-green	..	..	16·00	10·00
183	5s. purple	..	..	10·00	7·00
184	10s. grey	..	..	23·00	15·00
185	£1 black	..	..	25·00	17·00
172/185			Set of 14	£130	55·00

Designs:—Horiz—1d. *Fitzroy* (supply ship); 2d. Magellan Goose; 2½d. Map of Falkland Islands; 4d. Auster Autocrat aircraft; 6d. *John Biscoe I* (research ship); 9d. View of the Two Sisters; 1s. 3d. Kelp goose and gander; 10s. Southern Sealion and South American Fur Seal; £1 Hulk of *Great Britain*. Vert—1s. Gentoo Penguins; 2s. 6d. Sheep-shearing; 5s. Battle Memorial.

44 Queen Elizabeth II

(Des and eng B.W. Recess D.L.R.)

1953 (4 June). *Coronation. Wmk Mult Script CA. P* 13½×13.
186	**44**	1d. black and scarlet	..	..	80	1·25

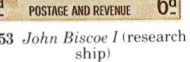
53 *John Biscoe I* (research ship)

54 Austral Thrush

(Recess Waterlow)

1955–57. *Designs previously used for King George VI issue but with portrait of Queen Elizabeth II as in T* **53**. *Wmk Mult Script CA. P* 13 × 13½ *(vert) or* 13½ × 13 *(horiz).*
187	½d. green (2.9.57)	..	..	70	1·25
188	1d. scarlet (2.9.57)	..	..	1·25	1·00
189	2d. violet (3.9.56)	..	..	3·25	4·50
190	6d. deep yellow-brown (1.6.55)		..	6·50	60
191	9d. orange-yellow (2.9.57)	..	..	17·00	17·00
192	1s. black (15.7.57)	..	..	6·00	1·25
187/92	..	..	Set of 6	30·00	23·00

Designs: *Horiz*—½d. Sheep; 1d. *Fitzroy* (supply ship); 9d. Magellan Goose; 9d. View of Two Sisters. *Vert*—1s. Gentoo Penguins.

(Des from sketches by S. Scott. Recess Waterlow, then D.L.R. (from 9.1.62 onwards))

1960 (10 Feb)–**66**. *T* **54** *and similar horiz designs. W w 12 (upright). P* 13½.
193	½d. black and myrtle-green	..	4·50	50
	a. *Black and green* (DLR) (9.1.62)		13·00	4·50
	aw. Wmk inverted		£2250	£1100
194	1d. black and scarlet	..		1·75	80
	a. *Black and carmine-red* (DLR) (15.7.63)	10·00	3·75
195	2d. black and blue	..		4·00	1·00
	a. *Black and deep blue* (DLR) (25.10.66)	17·00	15·00
196	2½d. black and yellow-brown		..	1·50	30
197	3d. black and olive	..		80	30
198	4d. black and carmine	..		1·25	75
199	5½d. black and violet	..		2·25	2·00
200	6d. black and sepia	..		2·50	30
201	9d. black and orange-red	..		2·25	90
202	1s. black and maroon	..		80	30
203	1s. 3d. black and ultramarine		..	10·00	13·00
204	2s. black and brown-red	..		27·00	2·50
	a. *Black and lake-brown* (DLR) (25.10.66)	£120	42·00
205	5s. black and turquoise	..		27·00	11·00
206	10s. black and purple	..		48·00	13·00
207	£1 black and orange-yellow	..		48·00	27·00
193/207	..	..	..	Set of 15	£150	65·00

Designs:—1d. Southern Black-backed Gull; 2d. Gentoo Penguins; 2½d. Long-tailed Meadowlark; 3d. Magellan Geese; 4d. Falkland Islands Flightless Steamer Ducks; 5½d. Rockhopper Penguin; 6d. Black-browed Albatross; 9d. Silvery Grebe; 1s. Magellanic Oystercatchers; 1s. 3d. Chilean Teal; 2s. Kelp Geese; 5s. King Cormorants; 10s. Common Caracara; £1 Black-necked Swan.

Waterlow

De La Rue

Waterlow printings were from Frame Plates 1 or 2. The De La Rue printings of the ½d., 1d., 2d. and 2s. are all from Frame Plate 2 and can be distinguished by the finer lines of shading on the Queen's face, neck and shoulders (appearing as a white face) and also the very faint cross hatching left of the face. Apart from this the shades differ in varying degrees. Frame Plate 1 was used by De La Rue to print initial supplies of the 6d. and these stamps have little to distinguish them from the original printing. Frame Plate 2 was subsequently used for this value which, although it shows the usual plate characteristics, does not differ in shade from the Waterlow printing.

For the ½d. with watermark sideways see No. 227.

NEW INFORMATION

The editor is always interested to correspond with people who have new information that will improve or correct the Catalogue.

1962   Falkland Islands — 7

69 Morse Key   70 One-valve Receiver

(Des M. Goaman. Photo Enschedé)

1962 (5 Oct). *50th Anniv of Establishment of Radio Communications.* T 69/70 *and similar vert design.* W w **12**. P 11½ × 11
208	69	6d. carmine-lake and orange	..	1·00	30
209	70	1s. deep bluish green and yellow-olive		1·25	35
210	—	2s. deep violet and ultramarine		1·25	1·50
		w. Wmk inverted	..	55·00	
208/10		.. .. ..	Set of 3	3·25	1·90

Design:—2s. Rotary Spark Transmitter.

70a Protein Foods   71 Red Cross Emblem

(Des M. Goaman. Photo Harrison)

1963 (4 June). *Freedom from Hunger.* W w **12**. P 14×14½.
211   70a   1s. ultramarine   ..   ..   13·00   1·50

(Des V. Whiteley. Litho B.W.)

1963 (2 Sept). *Red Cross Centenary.* W w **12**. P 13½.
212	71	1d. red and black	..	5·00	50
213		1s. red and blue	..	20·00	6·00

71a Shakespeare and Memorial
Theatre, Stratford-upon-Avon

(Des R. Granger Barrett. Photo Harrison)

1964 (23 Apr). *400th Birth Anniv of William Shakespeare.* W w **12**. P 14×14½.
214   71a   6d. black   ..   ..   ..   1·25   50

72 H.M.S. *Glasgow*

(Recess D.L.R.)

1964 (8 Dec)   *50th Anniv of the Battle of the Falkland Islands.* T **72** *and similar designs.* W w **12**. P 13 × 14 (2s.) or 13 (*others*).
215		2½d. black and red	..	10·00	3·25
216		6d. black and light blue	..	75	25
	a.	Centre Type **72**	..	£17000	
217		1s. black and carmine-red	..	75	1·00
	w.	Wmk inverted	..	£1100	
218		2s. black and blue	..	50	75
215/18			Set of 4	11·00	4·75

Designs: *Horiz*—6d. H.M.S. *Kent*; 1s. H.M.S. *Invincible*. *Vert*—2s. Battle Memorial.

It is believed that No. 216a came from a sheet which was first printed with the centre of the 2½d. and then accidentally included among the supply of the 6d. value and thus received the wrong frame. There have been seventeen reports of stamps showing the error, although it is believed that some of these *may* refer to the same example.

73 I.T.U. Emblem

(Des M. Goaman. Litho Enschedé)

1965 (26 May).   *I.T.U. Centenary.* W w **12**. P 11×11½.
219	73	1d. light blue and deep blue	..	75	30
		w. Wmk inverted	..	£550	
220		2s. lilac and bistre-yellow	..	9·00	1·75

74 I.C.Y. Emblem

(Des V. Whiteley. Litho Harrison)

1965 (25 Oct). *International Co-operation Year.* W w **12**. P 14½.
221	74	1d. reddish purple and turquoise-green	2·00	20
222		1s. deep bluish green and lavender	..	7·50	1·10

75 Sir Winston Churchill and
St. Paul's Cathedral in Wartime

(Des Jennifer Toombs. Photo Harrison)

1966 (24 Jan).   *Churchill Commemoration. Printed in black, cerise and gold with background in colours stated.* W w **12**. P 14.
223	75	½d. new blue	..	..	65	75
224		1d. deep green	..	..	2·25	15
		w. Wmk inverted	..	..	6·50	
225		1s. brown	..	..	7·00	2·00
		w. Wmk inverted	..	..	60·00	
226		2s. bluish violet	..	..	5·50	2·00
223/6		.. ..	Set of 4	14·00	4·50

8 — Falkland Islands   1966

1966 (25 Oct). *As No. 193a, but wmk* w *12 sideways.*
227   54   ½d. black and green   30   40

| 76 Globe and Human Rights Emblem | 77 Dusty Miller |

(Des M. Farrar Bell. Photo Harrison)

1968 (4 July). *Human Rights Year.* w *12. P* 14 × 14½.
228   76   2d. multicoloured   60   20
        a. Yellow omitted ("1968" white)   ..   £950
229   6d. muticoloured   70   20
230   1s. multicoloured   70   20
231   2s. multicoloured   70   30
228/31   ..   ..   ..   Set of 4   2·40   80

(Des Sylvia Goaman)

1968 (9 Oct). *Flowers. Designs as T 77. Chalk-surfaced paper.* W w *12 (sideways on vert designs). P* 14.
232   ½d. multicoloured   15   1·75
233   1½d. multicoloured   40   15
234   2d. multicoloured   50   15
235   3d. multicoloured   ..   ..   5·50   75
236   3½d. multicoloured   30   30
237   4½d. multicoloured   ..   ..   1·50   2·00
238   5½d. olive-green, brown and yellow-green   1·50   2·00
239   6d. carmine, black and yellow-green   ..   75   20
240   1s. multicoloured   75   1·25
      w. Wmk inverted   ..   ..   85·00
241   1s. 6d. multicoloured   ..   ..   4·50   12·00
242   2s. multicoloured   ..   ..   5·50   6·50
243   3s. multicoloured   ..   ..   8·00   8·00
244   5s. multicoloured   ..   ..   28·00   13·00
245   £1 multicoloured   ..   ..   13·00   2·00
232/45   ..   ..   ..   Set of 14   65·00   45·00
  Designs: *Horiz*—1½d. Pig Vine; 3½d. Sea Cabbage; 5½d. Arrowleaf Marigold; 6d. Diddle Dee; 1s. Scurvy Grass; 5s. Felton's Flower. *Vert*—2d. Pale Maiden; 3d. Dog Orchid; 4½d. Vanilla Daisy; 1s. 6d. Prickly Burr; 2s. Fachine; 3s. Lavender; £1 Yellow Orchid.
  A further printing of the £1 took place with the decimal surcharges issued 15 February 1971. It was for some time believed that stamps from this printing could be identified by the brown shading which extended to the foot of the design, instead of stopping short as on the original printing, but this test has now been shown to be inconsistent.
  For stamps inscribed in decimal currency see Nos. 276/88, 293/5 and 315.

91 De Havilland D.H.C.2 Beaver Seaplane

(Des V. Whiteley. Litho Format)

1969 (8 Apr). *21st Anniv of Government Air Services. T 91 and similar horiz designs. Multicoloured.* W w *12 (sideways). P* 14.
246   2d. Type 91   35   30
247   6d. Noorduyn Norseman V   ..   40   35
248   1s. Auster Autocrat   50   35
249   2s. Falkland Islands Arms   ..   1·50   2·00
246/9   ..   ..   ..   Set of 4   2·50   2·75

92 Holy Trinity Church, 1869

(Des G. Drummond. Litho Format)

1969 (30 Oct). *Centenary of Bishop Stirling's Consecration. T 92 and similar horiz designs.* W w *12 (sideways). P* 14.
250   2d. black, grey and apple-green   50   60
251   6d. black, grey and orange-red   50   60
252   1s. black, grey and lilac   50   60
253   2s. multicoloured   70   75
250/3   ..   ..   ..   Set of 4   2·00   2·25
  Designs:—6d. Christ Church Cathedral, 1969; 1s. Bishop Stirling; 2s. Bishop's Mitre.

| 96 Mounted Volunteer | 97 S.S. *Great Britain* (1843) |

(Des R. Granger Barrett. Litho B.W.)

1970 (30 Apr). *Golden Jubilee of Defence Force. T 96 and similar designs. Multicoloured.* W w *12 (sideways on 2d. and 1s.). P* 13.
254   2d. Type 96   ..   ..   1·90   70
255   6d. Defence Post (*horiz*)   ..   2·00   70
256   1s. Corporal in Number One Dress Uniform   2·00   70
257   2s. Defence Force Badge (*horiz*)   ..   3·00   75
254/7   ..   ..   ..   Set of 4   8·00   2·50

(Des V. Whiteley. Litho J.W.)

1970 (30 Oct). *Restoration of S.S. "Great Britain". T 97 and views of the ship at different dates. Multicoloured.* W w *12 (sideways*). P* 14½ × 14.
258   2d. Type 97   ..   ..   1·75   40
259   4d. In 1845   ..   ..   2·00   1·00
      w. Wmk Crown to right of CA   ..   15·00
260   9d. In 1876   ..   ..   2·00   1·00
261   1s. In 1886   ..   ..   2·00   1·00
      w. Wmk Crown to right of CA   ..   £700
262   2s. In 1970   ..   ..   2·00   1·00
258/62   ..   ..   ..   Set of 5   8·75   4·00
  *The normal sideways watermark shows Crown to left of CA, as seen from the back of the stamp.

99 Dusty Miller

1971 (15 Feb). *Decimal Currency. Nos. 232/44 surch as T* **98**. W w **12** (*sideways on vert designs*). *P* 14.

263	½p. on ½d. multicoloured		25	20
264	1p. on 1½d. multicoloured		30	15
	a. Error. Surch 5p.		£400	
	b. Do. but surch at right		£1000	
	c. Surch albino		£110	
	d. Surch albino in pair with normal		£3250	
265	1½p. on 2d. multicoloured		30	15
266	2p. on 3d. multicoloured		50	20
267	2½p. on 3½d. multicoloured		30	20
268	3p. on 4½d. multicoloured		30	20
269	4p. on 5½d. olive-yellow, brown & yell-grn		30	20
270	5p. on 6d. carmine, black and yellow-green		30	20
271	6p. on 1s. multicoloured		8·00	5·50
272	7½p. on 1s. 6d. multicoloured		8·00	6·50
273	10p. on 2s. multicoloured		8·50	3·00
274	15p. on 3s. multicoloured		6·50	2·75
275	25p. on 5s. multicoloured		7·00	3·25
263/75		Set of 13	35·00	20·00

1972 (1 June). *As Nos. 232/44, but Glazed, ordinary paper and with values inscr in decimal currency as T* **99**. W w **12** (*sideways on* ½, 1½, 2, 3, 7½, 10 *and* 15p.). *P* 14.

276	½p. multicoloured		35	4·25
277	1p. multicoloured (as 1½d.)		30	40
278	1½p. multicoloured (as 2d.)		30	3·75
279	2p. multicoloured (as 3d.)		13·00	1·25
280	2½p. multicoloured (as 3½d.)		35	3·75
281	3p. multicoloured (as 4½d.)		35	1·25
282	4p. olive-yellow, brown & yell-grn (as 5½d.)		40	50
283	5p. carmine, black and yellow-green (as 6d.)		40	55
284	6p. multicoloured (as 1s.)		20·00	9·50
285	7½p. multicoloured (as 1s. 6d.)		1·50	4·00
286	10p. multicoloured (as 2s.)		9·00	4·50
287	15p. multicoloured (as 3s.)		4·50	5·00
288	25p. multicoloured (as 5s.)		4·50	6·00
276/88		Set of 13	48·00	35·00

See also Nos. 293/5 and 315.

100 Romney Marsh Sheep and Southern Sealions

(Des (from photograph by D. Groves) and photo Harrison)

1972 (20 Nov). *Royal Silver Wedding. Multicoloured; background colour given.* W w **12**. *P* 14 × 14½.

289	**100**	1p. grey-green	40	40
290		10p. bright blue	85	85

100a Princess Anne and Captain Mark Phillips

1973 (14 Nov). *Royal Wedding. Centre multicoloured.* W w **12** (*sideways*). *P* 13½.

291	**100a**	5p. bright mauve	25	10
292		15p. brown-ochre	35	20

(Des PAD Studio. Litho Questa)

1974 (25 Feb–18 Oct). *As Nos. 276, 279 and 284, but wmk upright on* ½p. *and* 2p. *and sideways* on* 6p. *P* 14.

293	½p. multicoloured (18.10.74)		12·00	28·00
	w. Wmk inverted		£190	
294	2p. multicoloured		23·00	3·25
	w. Wmk inverted		£350	
295	6p. multicoloured (28.3.74)		1·50	2·25
	w. Wmk Crown to right of CA		£425	
293/5		Set of 3	32·00	30·00

*The normal sideways watermark shows Crown to left of CA, *as seen from the back of the stamp.*

101 South American Fur Seal   **102** 19th-Century Mail-coach

(Des J. Cooter. Litho Walsall)

1974 (6 Mar). *Tourism. T* **101** *and similar horiz designs. Multicoloured.* W w **12**. *P* 14.

296	2p. Type **101**		2·25	1·25
297	4p. Trout-fishing		3·00	1·25
298	5p. Rockhopper penguins		9·50	2·50
299	15p. Long-tailed Meadowlark		12·00	4·50
296/9		Set of 4	24·00	8·50

(Des PAD Studio. Litho Questa)

1974 (31 July). *Centenary of Universal Postal Union. T* **102** *and similar vert designs. Multicoloured.* W w **12** (*sideways*). *P* 14.

300	2p. Type **102**		25	25
301	5p. Packet ship, 1841		35	45
302	8p. First U.K. aerial post, 1911		40	55
303	16p. Ship's catapult mail, 1920's		60	75
300/3		Set of 4	1·40	1·75

103 Churchill and Houses of Parliament

(Des G. Vasarhelyi. Litho Enschedé)

1974 (30 Nov). *Birth Centenary of Sir Winston Churchill. T* **103** *and similar horiz design. Multicoloured.* W w **12**. *P* 13½.

304	16p. Type **103**		1·40	1·60
305	20p. Churchill with H.M.S. *Inflexible* and H.M.S. *Invincible*, 1914		1·40	1·90
MS306	108×83 mm. Nos. 304/5		8·00	7·00
	w. Wmk inverted		£170	

10 — Falkland Islands   1974

104 H.M.S. *Exeter*   **105** Seal and Flag Badge

(Des J.W. Litho Harrison)

1974 (13 Dec). *35th Anniv of the Battle of the River Plate.* T **104** *and similar horiz designs. Multicoloured.* W w **14** *(sideways*).* P 14.

307	2p. Type **104**			3·00	1·60
	w. Wmk Crown to right of CA			13·00	6·00
308	6p. H.M.N.Z.S. *Achilles*			4·50	3·50
	w. Wmk Crown to right of CA			8·50	3·50
309	8p. *Admiral Graf Spee*			5·00	4·50
	w. Wmk Crown to right of CA			95·00	50·00
310	16p. H.M.S. *Ajax*			8·50	15·00
	w. Wmk Crown to right of CA			27·00	17·00
307/10			Set of 4	19·00	22·00

*The normal sideways watermark shows Crown to left of CA, as seen from the back of the stamp.

(Des PAD Studio. Litho Walsall)

1975 (28 Oct). *50th Anniv of Heraldic Arms.* T **105** *and similar vert designs. Multicoloured.* W w **14** (*inverted*). P 14.

311	2p. Type **105**			80	35
312	7½p. Coat of arms, 1925			1·60	1·40
313	10p. Coat of arms, 1948			1·75	1·60
314	16p. Arms of the Dependencies, 1952			2·50	3·25
311/14			Set of 4	6·00	6·00

1975 (8 Dec). *As No. 276 but* W w **14** *(sideways).* P 14.
315 99 ½p. multicoloured .. .. 2·25 3·50

106 ½p. Coin and Brown Trout

(Des G. Drummond. Litho Questa)

1975 (31 Dec). *New Coinage.* T **106** *and similar horiz designs each showing coin. Multicoloured.* W w **12** *(sideways).* P 14.

316	2p. Type **106**			90	50
	w. Wmk Crown to right of CA			65·00	
317	5½p. Gentoo Penguin and 1p. coin			1·40	1·50
318	8p. Magellan Goose and 2p. coin			1·75	1·75
319	10p. Black-browed Albatross and 5p. coin			1·90	2·00
320	16p. Southern Sealion and 10p. coin			2·25	2·50
316/20			Set of 5	7·50	7·50

*The normal sideways watermark shows Crown to left of CA, as seen from the back of the stamp.

107 Gathering Sheep

(Des PAD Studio. Litho J.W.)

1976 (28 Apr). *Sheep Farming Industry.* T **107** *and similar horiz designs. Multicoloured.* W w **14** *(sideways).* P 13½.

321	2p. Type **107**			65	40
322	7½p. Shearing			1·40	1·50
323	10p. Dipping			1·75	1·60
324	20p. Shipping			2·25	3·00
321/4			Set of 4	5·50	6·00

108 The Queen awaiting Anointment

(Des M. and G. Shamir; adapted J.W. Litho Questa)

1977 (7 Feb–1 Nov). *Silver Jubilee.* T **108** *and similar horiz designs. Multicoloured.* P 13½. (*a*) W w **14** *(sideways).*

325	6p. Visit of Prince Philip, 1957			2·00	1·25
326	11p. Queen Elizabeth, ampulla and anointing spoon			30	75
	a. Booklet pane of 4 with blank margins (1.11.77)			75	
327	33p. Type **108**			40	1·25
	a. Booklet pane of 4 with blank margins (1.11.77)			1·00	

(*b*) W w **12** *(sideways) (from booklets only)* (1.11.77)

327b	6p. Visit of Prince Philip,1957			2·75	4·00
	ba. Booklet pane of 4 with blank margins			10·00	
325/7b			Set of 4	5·00	6·50

109 Map of Falkland Islands

(Des K. Penny. Litho Questa)

1977 (24 Oct). *Telecommunications.* T **109** *and similar horiz designs. Multicoloured.* W w **14** *(sideways).* P 14½.

328	3p. Type **109**			75	15
329	11p. Ship to shore communications			1·25	40
	w. Wmk Crown to right of CA			£110	
330	40p. Telex and telephone service			2·75	1·75
328/30			Set of 3	4·25	2·10

*The normal sideways watermark shows Crown to left of CA, as seen from the back of the stamp.

110 *A.E.S.,* 1957–74

(Des J. Smith; adapted R. Granger Barrett. Litho Questa)

1978 (25 Jan)–**82**. *Mail Ships. Horiz designs as* T **110**. *Multicoloured.* W w **14** *(sideways).* P 14. A. *Without imprint date.*

331A	1p. Type **110**			20	30
332A	2p. *Darwin,* 1957–73			30	30
333A	3p. *Merak-N.,* 1951–2			25	90
	w. Wmk Crown to right of CA			£200	
334A	4p. *Fitzroy,* 1936–57			30	40

1978 FALKLAND ISLANDS — 11

335A	5p. *Lafonia*, 1936–41	..	..	30	30
336A	6p. *Fleurus*, 1924–33	..	..	30	40
337A	7p. *Falkland*, 1914–34	..	..	30	1·50
338A	8p. *Oravia*, 1900–12	..	..	35	50
339A	9p. *Memphis*, 1890–97	..	..	35	50
340A	10p. *Black Hawk*, 1873–80	..	..	35	50
341A	20p. *Foam*, 1863–72	..	..	1·75	1·50
342A	25p. *Fairy*, 1857–61	..	..	2·00	3·00
343A	50p. *Amelia*, 1852–54	..	..	2·25	4·00
	w. Wmk Crown to right of CA			£275	
344A	£1 *Nautilus*, 1846–48	..	..	4·00	7·00
345A	£3 *Hebe*, 1842–46	..	..	11·00	16·00
331A/45A			Set of 15	21·00	32·00

B. *With imprint date ("1982") at foot* (1.12.82†)

331B	1p. Type **110**	..	..	45	1·50
332B	2p. *Darwin*, 1957–73	..	..	50	1·50
333B	3p. *Merak-N.*, 1951–2	..	..	65	1·50
334B	4p. *Fitzroy*, 1936–57	..	..	65	1·50
335B	5p. *Lafonia*, 1936–41	..	..	65	1·50
336B	6p. *Fleurus*, 1924–33	..	..	65	1·50
337B	7p. *Falkland*, 1914–34	..	..	70	1·50
338B	8p. *Oravia*, 1900–12	..	..	70	1·50
339B	9p. *Memphis*, 1890–97	..	..	70	1·50
340B	10p. *Black Hawk*, 1873–80	..	..	70	1·50
341B	20p. *Foam*, 1863–72	..	..	1·25	2·00
342B	25p. *Fairy*, 1857–61	..	..	1·25	2·50
343B	50p. *Amelia*, 1852–54	..	..	2·25	3·00
344B	£1 *Nautilus*, 1846–48	..	..	2·50	4·50
345B	£3 *Hebe*, 1842–46	..	..	5·50	9·50
331B/45B			Set of 15	17·00	32·00

*The normal sideways watermark shows Crown to left of CA, as seen from the back of the stamp.

†Nos. 331B/45B were available from the Crown Agents in London on 13 July 1982.

111 Short Hythe at Stanley

(Des L. McCombie. Litho Walsall)

1978 (28 Apr). *26th Anniv of First Direct Flight, Southampton–Port Stanley. T **111** and similar horiz design. Multicoloured. W w 14 (sideways). P 14.*

346	11p. Type **111**	..	..	3·00	2·50
347	33p. Route map and Short Hythe		..	3·50	3·00

112 Red Dragon of Wales   **113** First Fox Bay P.O. and 1d. Stamp of 1878

(Des C. Abbott. Litho Questa)

1978 (2 June). *25th Anniv of Coronation. T **112** and similar vert designs. P 15.*

348	25p. bistre, bright blue and silver	..	..	60	1·00
	a. Sheetlet. Nos. 348/50 × 2		..	3·00	
349	25p. multicoloured	..	..	60	1·00
350	25p. bistre, bright blue and silver	..	..	60	1·00
348/50			Set of 3	1·60	2·75

Designs:—No. 348, Type **112**; No. 349, Queen Elizabeth II; No. 350, Hornless Ram.

Nos. 348/50 were printed together in small sheets of 6, containing two *se-tenant* strips of 3, with horizontal gutter margin between.

(Des J. Cooter. Litho B.W.)

1978 (8 Aug). *Centenary of First Falkland Is Postage Stamps. T **113** and similar vert designs. Multicoloured. W w 14. P 13½ × 13.*

351	3p. Type **113**	..	..	25	20
352	11p. Second Stanley P.O. and 4d. stamp of 1879			40	50
353	15p. New Island P.O. and 6d. stamp of 1878			50	60
	w. Wmk inverted	..	..	£700	
354	22p. First Stanley P.O. and 1s. stamp of 1878	..	..	80	1·00
351/4			Set of 4	1·75	2·10

114 *Macrocystis pyrifera*   **115** Britten Norman Islander over Falkland Islands

(Des I. Strange. Litho Questa)

1979 (19 Feb). *Kelp and Seaweed. T **114** and similar multi-coloured designs. W w 14 (sideways on 11 and 15p). P 14.*

355	3p. Type **114**	..	..	30	25
356	7p. *Durvillea* sp	..	..	50	45
357	11p. *Lessonia* sp (*horiz*)	..	..	65	60
358	15p. *Callophyllis* sp (*horiz*)	..	..	85	80
359	25p. *Iradaea* sp	..	..	1·00	1·40
355/9	..		Set of 5	3·00	3·25

(Des G. Hutchins. Litho Rosenbaum Bros, Vienna)

1979 (1 May). *Opening of Stanley Airport. T **115** and similar horiz designs showing diagrammatic drawings. Multi-coloured. W w 14 (sideways*). P 13½.*

360	3p. Type **115**	..	..	40	20
	w. Wmk Crown to right of CA	..	35·00		
361	11p. Fokker F.27 Friendship over South Atlantic			80	60
	w. Wmk Crown to left of CA	..	55·00		
362	15p. Fokker F.28 Fellowship over Airport			90	60
	w. Wmk Crown to left of CA	..	40·00		
363	25p. Cessna 172 Skyhawk, Britten Norman Islander, Fokker F.27 Friendship and Fokker F.28 Fellowship over runway			1·50	80
	w. Wmk Crown to left of CA	..	3·75		
360/3			Set of 4	3·25	2·00

*The normal sideways watermark shows Crown to left of CA on the 3p. and Crown to right of CA on the other values, all as seen from the back of the stamp.

116 Sir Rowland Hill and 1953 Coronation 1d. Commemorative

(Des J.W. Litho Questa)

1979 (27 Aug). *Death Centenary of Sir Rowland Hill. T **116** and similar multicoloured designs showing stamps and portrait. W w 14 (sideways* on 3 and 25p.). P 14.*

364	3p. Type **116**	..	..	25	25
	w. Wmk Crown to left of CA	..	..	2·00	
365	11p. 1878 1d. stamp (*vert*)	..	..	40	70

12 — Falkland Islands — 1979

366	25p. Penny Black			60	85
	w. Wmk Crown to left of CA			£200	
364/6			Set of 3	1·10	1·60
MS367	137×98 mm. 33p. 1916 5s. stamp (*vert*)			85	1·50

*The normal sideways watermark shows Crown to right of CA, *as seen from the back of the stamp*.

117 Mail Drop by De Havilland D.H.C.2 Beaver Aircraft

118 Peale's Dolphin

(Des A. Peake; adapted J.W. Litho Questa)

1979 (26 Nov). *Centenary of U.P.U. Membership.* T **117** *and similar horiz designs. Multicoloured.* W w **14** (*sideways**).* P 14.

368	3p. Type **117**			20	20
	w. Wmk Crown to right of CA			2·00	
369	11p. Mail by horseback			45	55
370	25p. Mail by schooner *Gwendolin*			75	1·00
368/70			Set of 3	1·25	1·60

*The normal sideways watermark shows Crown to left of CA, *as seen from the back of the stamp*.

(Des I. Strange. Litho Harrison)

1980 (25 Feb). *Dolphins and Porpoises.* T **118** *and similar designs.* W w **14** (*sideways** *on 6, 7, 15 and 25p.).* P 14.

371	3p. black, chestnut and blue			45	45
	w. Inverted			£200	
372	6p. multicoloured			55	55
373	7p. multicoloured			55	55
374	11p. black, new blue and rose-red			80	90
375	15p. black, chestnut and greyish blue			90	1·10
	w. Wmk Crown to right of CA			60·00	
376	25p. multicoloured			1·00	1·75
371/6			Set of 6	3·75	4·75

Designs: *Horiz*—6p. Commerson's Dolphin; 7p. Hourglass Dolphin; 15p. Dusky Dolphin; 25p. Killer Whale. *Vert*—11p. Spectacled Porpoise.

*The normal sideways watermark shows Crown to left of CA, *as seen from the back of the stamp*.

119 1878 Falkland Islands Postmark

(Des G. Hutchins. Litho Walsall)

1980 (6 May). *"London 1980" International Stamp Exhibition.* T **119** *and similar horiz designs showing postmarks.* W w **14** (*sideways*). P 14.

377	11p. black, gold and light blue			30	30
	a. Block of 6. Nos. 377/82			1·50	
378	11p. black, gold and greenish yellow			30	30
379	11p. black, gold and blue-green			30	30
380	11p. black, gold and pale violet			30	30
381	11p. black, gold and claret			30	30
382	11p. black, gold and flesh			30	30
377/82			Set of 6	1·50	1·50

Designs:—No. 377, Type **119**; No. 378, 1915 New Island; No. 379, 1901 Falkland Islands; No. 380, 1935 Port Stanley; No. 381, 1952 Port Stanley first overseas airmail; No. 382, 1934 Fox Bay.

Nos. 377/82 were printed together, *se-tenant*, as a sheetlet, containing one of each design.

120 Queen Elizabeth the Queen Mother at Ascot, 1971

(Des Harrison. Litho Questa)

1980 (4 Aug). *80th Birthday of Queen Elizabeth the Queen Mother.* W w **14** (*sideways*). P 14.

383	120	11p. multicoloured			40	30

121 Forster's Caracara

(Des I. Strange. Litho Secura, Singapore)

1980 (11 Aug). *Birds of Prey.* T **121** *and similar horiz designs. Multicoloured.* W w **14** (*sideways*). P 13×13½.

384	3p. Type **121**			70	25
	w. Wmk Crown to left of CA			3·25	
385	11p. Red-backed Buzzard			90	60
	w. Wmk Crown to left of CA			£350	
386	15p. Common Caracara			1·10	75
	w. Wmk Crown to left of CA			£400	
387	25p. Peregrine Falcon			1·25	1·00
	w. Wmk Crown to left of CA			1·25	
384/7			Set of 4	3·50	2·40

*The normal sideways watermark shows Crown to right of CA, *as seen from the back of the stamp*.

122 Stanley

(Des C. Abbott. Litho Rosenbaum Bros, Vienna)

1981 (7 Jan). *Early Settlements.* T **122** *and similar horiz designs. Multicoloured.* W w **14** (*sideways**). P 14.

388	3p. Type **122**			15	15
389	11p. Port Egmont			30	35
390	25p. Port Louis			60	65
	w. Wmk Crown to left of CA			£300	
391	33p. Mission House, Keppel Island			70	80
	w. Wmk Crown to left of CA			£250	
388/91			Set of 4	1·60	1·75

*The normal sideways watermark shows Crown to right of CA, *as seen from the back of the stamp*.

123 Sheep

1981   Falkland Islands — 13

(Des P. Oxenham. Litho Questa)

1981 (9 Jan). *Farm Animals. T* **123** *and similar horiz designs. Multicoloured. W* w **14** *(sideways*). P* 14.

392	3p. Type **123**	..	20	30
393	11p. Cattle	..	35	55
	w. Wmk Crown to right of CA	..	£140	
394	25p. Horse	..	70	1·25
	w. Wmk Crown to right of CA	..	80·00	
395	33p. Dogs	..	1·00	1·50
392/5		Set of 4	2·00	3·25

*The normal sideways watermark shows Crown to left of CA, as seen from the back of the stamp.

124 Bowles and Carver, 1779   125 Wedding Bouquet from Falkland Islands

(Des I. Strange. Litho Walsall)

1981 (22 May). *Early Maps. T* **124** *and similar horiz designs in black, dull rose and stone (26p.) or multicoloured (others). W* w **14** *(sideways*). P* 14.

396	3p. Type **124**	..	35	30
397	10p. J. Hawkesworth, 1773	..	55	55
	w. Wmk Crown to right of CA	..	£200	
398	13p. Eman. Bowen, 1747	..	60	75
399	15p. T. Boutflower, 1768	..	60	85
400	25p. Philippe de Pretot, 1771	..	65	90
401	26p. Bellin *Petite Atlas Maritime*, Paris, 1764	..	65	90
396/401		Set of 6	3·00	3·75

*The normal sideways watermark shows Crown to left of CA, as seen from the back of the stamp.

(Des and litho J.W.)

1981 (22 July). *Royal Wedding. T* **125** *and similar vert designs. Multicoloured. W* w **14**. *P* 13½ × 13.

402	10p. Type **125**	..	30	40
	w. Wmk inverted	..	65·00	
403	13p. Prince Charles riding	..	40	50
	w. Wmk inverted	..	35·00	
404	52p. Prince Charles and Lady Diana Spencer	..	70	1·00
402/4		Set of 3	1·25	1·75

 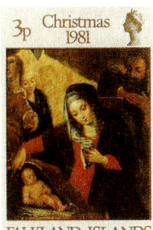

126 "Handicrafts"   127 "The Adoration of the Holy Child" (16th-century Dutch artist)

(Des BG Studio. Litho Questa)

1981 (28 Sept*). *25th Anniv of Duke of Edinburgh Award Scheme. T* **126** *and similar vert designs. Multicoloured. W* w **14**. *P* 14.

405	10p. Type **126**	..	15	20
406	13p. "Camping"	..	20	30
407	15p. "Canoeing"	..	30	40
408	26p. Duke of Edinburgh	..	35	60
405/8		Set of 4	90	1·40

*This is the local date of issue. The Crown Agents released the stamps in London on 14 September.

(Des BG Studio. Litho Walsall)

1981 (9 Nov*). *Christmas. Paintings. T* **127** *and similar vert designs. Multicoloured. W* w **14**. *P* 14.

409	3p. Type **127**	..	20	20
410	13p. "The Holy Family in an Italian Landscape" (17th-century Genoan artist)	..	35	45
411	26p. "The Holy Virgin" (Reni)	..	55	75
409/11		Set of 3	1·00	1·25

*This is the local date of issue. The Crown Agents released the stamps in London on 2 November.

128 Patagonian Sprat

(Des I. Strange. Litho Questa)

1981 (7 Dec). *Shelf Fishes. T* **128** *and similar multicoloured designs. W* w **14** *(sideways on* 5, 15 *and* 25p.*). P* 14 × 13½ (13, 26p.) *or* 13½ × 14 *(others).*

412	5p. Type **128**	..	20	20
413	13p. Gunther's Rockcod (*vert*)	..	35	35
414	15p. Argentine Hake	..	40	40
415	25p. Southern Blue Whiting	..	60	75
416	26p. Grey-tailed Skate (*vert*)	..	60	75
412/16		Set of 5	1·90	2·25

129 *Lady Elizabeth*, 1913

(Des J. Smith. Litho Questa)

1982 (15 Feb). *Shipwrecks. T* **129** *and similar horiz designs. Multicoloured. W* w **14** *(sideways). P* 14½.

417	5p. Type **129**	..	30	50
418	13p. *Capricorn*, 1882	..	35	70
419	15p. *Jhelum*, 1870	..	40	85
420	25p. *Snowsquall*, 1864	..	55	1·10
421	26p. *St. Mary*, 1890	..	55	1·10
417/21		Set of 5	1·90	3·75

ARGENTINE OCCUPATION
2 April to 15 June 1982

Following incidents, involving the illegal presence of Argentine scrap-metal workers on the dependency of South Georgia from 18 March 1982, Argentine forces attacked Port Stanley, the capital of the Falkland Islands early in the morning of 2 April. The small garrison of Royal Marines was overwhelmed and the Governor forced to agree to a cease-fire, before being deported.

South Georgia was occupied by the Argentines on the following day.

British forces, dispatched from the United Kingdom, recaptured South Georgia on 25 April, and, after landing at various points on East Falkland, forced the surrender of the Argentine troops throughout the islands on 15 June.

14 — Falkland Islands 1982

The last mail to be dispatched from the Falkland Islands prior to the invasion left on 31 March. The Port Stanley Post Office was closed on 2 April, when all current issues were withdrawn. From 5 April an Argentine post office operated in the town, initially accepting mail without stamps, which was then cancelled by a post-mark inscribed "ISLAS MALVINAS". Any letters tendered franked with Falkland Islands issues had these cancelled by ball-point pen. A limited range of Argentine stamps was placed on sale from 8 April. The Argentine definitive overprinted "LAS MALVINAS SON ARGENTINAS" for use throughout the country, was also available.

Following the Argentine surrender a rudimentary mail service was operating by 17 June, but the Port Stanley Post Office did not re-open until 24 July.

The last mail from South Georgia before the invasion was sent out on 16 March, although items remaining in the post office there were evacuated by the Deputy Postmaster when he was deported to the United Kingdom by the Argentines. The first mail left after recapture by the British on 2 May.

BRITISH ADMINISTRATION RESTORED

130 Charles Darwin

131 Falkland Islands Coat of Arms

(Des L. Curtis. Litho Questa)

1982 (5 July*)   150*th Anniv of Charles Darwin's Voyage. T* **130** *and similar horiz designs. Multicoloured.* W w 14 (*sideways*). P 14.
```
422    5p. Type 130..       ..    ..    ..    30    25
423   17p. Darwin's microscope     ..    ..    50    60
424   25p. Falkland Islands Wolf ("Warrah")   70    80
425   34p. H.M.S. Beagle     ..    ..    ..    95   1·10
      a. Pale brown (background to side panels)
         omitted       ..    ..    ..    ..  £800
422/5          ..    ..    Set of 4   2·25  2·50
```
*It was initially intended that these stamps were to be issued on 19 April. First Day covers were prepared, postmarked with this date, but, because of the Argentine invasion, the stamps were not actually released until 5 July. A postmark showing the actual date of issue was struck alongside the stamps on the First Day covers.

(Des C. Abbott. Litho J.W.)

1982 (16 Aug).   21*st Birthday of Princess of Wales. T* **131** *and similar vert designs. Multicoloured.* W w 14. P 13.
```
426    5p. Type 131 ..       ..    ..    ..    15    20
427   17p. Princess at Royal Opera House, Covent
           Garden, November 1981..    ..    30    40
428   37p. Bride and groom in doorway of St Paul's   50    70
429   50p. Formal portrait  ..    ..    ..    65    90
426/9 ..    ..    ..    ..    Set of 4    1·40   2·00
```

132 Map of Falkland Islands

(Des PAD Studio. Litho Format)

1982 (13 Sept).   *Rebuilding Fund.* W w 14 (*sideways**). P 11.
```
430   132    £1 + £1 multicoloured    ..    2·40   4·50
             w. Wmk Crown to right of CA       75·00
```
*The normal sideways watermark shows Crown to left of CA, as seen from the back of the stamp.

1st PARTICIPATION COMMONWEALTH GAMES 1982
(133)   134 Blackish Cincloides

1982 (7 Oct).   *Commonwealth Games, Brisbane. Nos.* 335B *and* 342B *optd with T* **133**.
```
431    5p. Lafonia, 1936–41    ..    ..    ..    15    30
432   25p. Fairy, 1857–61      ..    ..    ..    60   1·10
```

(Des I. Strange. Litho W. S. Cowells Ltd)

1982 (6 Dec).   *Birds of the Passerine Family.* T **134** *and similar vert designs. Multicoloured.* W w 14 (*inverted on* 10p.). P 15 × 14½.
```
433    5p. Type 134             ..    ..    ..    35    35
434   10p. Black-chinned Siskin ..    ..    45    45
            w. Wmk upright      ..    ..    40·00
435   13p. Short-billed Marsh Wren    ..    50    55
436   17p. Black-throated Finch  ..    ..    55    65
437   25p. Correndera Pipit     ..    ..    65    85
438   34p. Dark-faced Ground Tyrant   ..    75   1·10
433/8          ..    ..    Set of 6    2·75   3·50
```
Imperforate examples of all values, except the 34p., exist from printer's waste which escaped destruction. Some are known on unwatermarked paper with thick red lines across the face of the stamps.

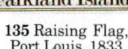
135 Raising Flag,   136 1933 British Administration
Port Louis, 1833   Centenary 3d. Commemorative

(Des I. Strange and J. Sheridan. Litho Questa)

1983 (3 Jan).   150*th Anniv of British Administration. T* **135** *and similar multicoloured designs.* W w 14 (*sideways on* 2, 10, 15, 25 *and* 50p.). P 14 × 13½ (1, 5, 20, 40p., £1, £2) *or* 13½ × 14 (*others*).
```
439    1p. Type 135             ..    ..    ..    20    30
440    2p. Chelsea pensioners and barracks, 1849
           (horiz)               ..    ..    30    40
441    5p. Development of wool trade, 1874   30    40
442   10p. Ship-repairing trade, 1850–1890 (horiz)  60  70
443   15p. Government House, early 20th century
           (horiz)               ..    ..    70    80
444   20p. Battle of Falkland Islands, 1914    90   1·25
445   25p. Whalebone Arch, 1933 (horiz) ..    90   1·25
446   40p. Contribution to War effort, 1939–45  1·40  1·60
447   50p. Duke of Edinburgh's visit, 1957 (horiz)  1·50  2·00
448    £1 Royal Marine uniforms ..    ..    2·00   3·00
449    £2 Queen Elizabeth II    ..    ..    2·75   4·50
439/49   ..    ..    ..    Set of 11   10·00  14·50
```

1983   Falkland Islands — 15

(Des L. Curtis. Litho Questa)

1983 (28 Mar*). *Commonwealth Day*. T **136** *and similar multicoloured designs*. W w **14** *(sideways on* 5p., 17p.). *P* 14.
450	5p. Type **136**	15	15
451	17p. 1933 British Administration Centenary ½d. commemorative	30	35
452	34p. 1933 British Administration Centenary 10s. commemorative (*vert*)	60	80
453	50p. 1983 British Administration 150th anniversary £2 commemorative (*vert*)	75	1·00
450/3	Set of 4	1·60	2·10

*This is the local date of issue: the Crown Agents released the stamps on 14 March.

137 British Army advancing across East Falkland

(Des A. Theobald. Litho Questa)

1983 (14 June). *First Anniv of Liberation*. T **137** *and similar horiz designs*. *Multicoloured*. W w **14** *(sideways)*. *P* 14.
454	5p. Type **137**	25	30
455	13p. S.S. *Canberra* and M.V. *Norland* at San Carlos	40	60
456	17p. R.A.F. Hawker Siddeley Harrier fighter	45	70
457	50p. H.M.S. *Hermes* (aircraft carrier)	1·00	1·40
454/7	Set of 4	1·90	2·75
MS458	169×130 mm. Nos. 454/7. P 12	2·25	3·50

138 Diddle Dee

(Des A. Chater. Litho Questa)

1983 (10 Oct). *Native Fruits*. T **138** *and similar horiz designs. Multicoloured*. W w **14** *(sideways)*. *P* 14.
459	5p. Type **138**	20	20
460	17p. Tea Berry	30	50
461	25p. Mountain Berry	45	65
462	34p. Native Strawberry	65	80
459/62	Set of 4	1·40	1·90

139 Britten Norman Islander

(Des Harrison. Litho Questa)

1983 (14 Nov). *Bicentenary of Manned Flight*. T **139** *and similar horiz designs. Multicoloured.* W w **14** *(sideways)*. *P* 14.
463	5p. Type **139**	15	20
464	13p. De Havilland D.H.C.2 Beaver	35	45
465	17p. Norduyn Norseman V	40	50
466	50p. Auster Autocrat	1·00	1·25
463/6	Set of 4	1·75	2·50

17 p

17 p

(140)   (140*a*)

1984 (3 Jan). Nos. 443 *and* 445 *surch as T* **140** *by Govt Printer, Port Stanley.*
467	17p. on 15p. Government House, early 20th century (figures as Type **140**)	60	45
	a. Surch figures as Type **140***a*	1·00	1·25
468	22p. on 25p. Whalebone Arch, 1933	65	55

The surcharge setting used for the 17p. contained 27 examples as Type **140** and 23 as Type **140***a*.

141 *Araneus cinnabarinus* (juvenile spider)   **142** *Wavertree* (sail merchantman)

(Des I. Strange. Litho Questa)

1984 (3 Jan)–**86**. *Insects and Spiders*. T **141** *and similar horiz designs. Multicoloured*. W w **14** *(sideways)*. *P* 14×14½.

A. *Without imprint date*
469A	1p. Type **141**	20	80
		2·00	2·00
470A	2p. *Alopophion occidentalis* (fly)	40	80
471A	3p. *Pareuxoina falkandica* (moth)	30	80
472A	4p. *Lissopterus quadrinotatus* (beetle)	30	80
473A	5p. *Issoria cytheris* (butterfly)	30	80
474A	6p. *Araneus cinnabarinus* (adult spider)	30	65
475A	7p. *Trachysphyrus penai* (fly)	30	65
476A	8p. *Caphornia ochricraspia* (moth)	30	65
477A	9p. *Caneorhinus biangulatus* (weevil)	30	65
478A	10p. *Syrphus octomaculatus* (fly)	30	65
479A	20p. *Malvinius compressiventris* (weevil)	2·25	75
480A	25p. *Metius blandus* (beetle)	75	90
481A	50p. *Parudenus falkandicus* (cricket)	1·00	1·50
482A	£1 *Emmenomma beauchenieus* (spider)	1·75	2·25
483A	£3 *Cynthia carye* (butterfly)	4·00	6·00
469A/83A	Set of 15	13·00	18·00

B. *With "1986" imprint date at foot of design*
470B	2p. *Alopophion occidentalis* (fly) (19.5.86)	2·75	2·75

(Des A. Theobald. Litho Questa)

1984 (7 May). *250th Anniv of "Lloyd's List" (newspaper)*. T **142** *and similar vert designs. Multicoloured.* W w **14**. *P* 14½ × 14.
484	6p. Type **142**	55	40
485	17p. *Bjerk* (whale catcher) at Port Stanley	1·10	60
486	22p. *Oravia* (liner) stranded	1·10	65
487	52p. *Cunard Countess* (liner)	1·60	2·00
484/7	Set of 4	3·75	3·25

NEW INFORMATION

The editor is always interested to correspond with people who have new information that will improve or correct the Catalogue.

16 — Falkland Islands   1984

143 Ship, Lockheed C-130 Hercules Aircraft and U.P.U. Logo

144 Great Grebe

(Des E. Nisbet, adapted L. Curtis. Litho Questa)

1984 (25 June). *Universal Postal Union Congress, Hamburg.* W w **14** (*sideways*). P 14.
488 143 22p. multicoloured 55 75

(Des I. Strange. Litho Questa)

1984 (6 Aug). *Grebes.* T **144** *and similar vert designs. Multicoloured.* W w **14**. P 14½.
489 17p. Type **144** .... 1·40 1·25
490 22p. Silvery Grebe .... 1·60 1·40
491 52p. White-tufted Grebe .... 3·00 4·75
489/91 .... Set of 3 5·50 6·75

145 Black-browed Albatross

146 Technical Drawing of Class "Wren" Locomotive

(Des I. Strange. Litho Questa)

1984 (5 Nov). *Nature Conservation.* T **145** *and similar vert designs. Multicoloured.* W w **14**. P 14½ × 14.
492 6p. Type **145** .... 1·25 80
493 17p. Tussock grass .... 1·25 1·10
494 22p. Dusky Dolphin and Southern Sealion 1·40 1·40
495 52p. Rockcod (fish) and krill .. 2·00 3·00
492/5 .... Set of 4 5·50 5·50
MS496 130×90 mm. Nos. 492/5 .... 5·50 7·00

(Des C. Abbott. Litho Questa)

1985 (18 Feb). *70th Anniv of Camber Railway.* T **146** *and similar horiz designs, each black, deep brown and pale cinnamon.* W w **14** (*sideways*). P 14.
497 7p. Type **146** 35 30
498 22p. Sail-propelled trolley ... 60 90
499 27p. Class "Wren" locomotive at work 65 1·25
500 54p. "Falkland Islands Express" passenger train (75×25 mm) .. 1·10 2·00
497/500 .... Set of 4 2·40 4·00

147 Construction Workers' Camp

148 The Queen Mother on 84th Birthday

(Des N. Shewring. Litho Questa)

1985 (12 May). *Opening of Mount Pleasant Airport.* T **147** *and similar horiz designs. Multicoloured.* W w **16** (*sideways*). P 14½ × 14.
501 7p. Type **147** 75 40
502 22p. Building construction .... 1·40 90
503 27p. Completed airport ...... 1·60 1·10
504 54p. Lockheed L-1011 TriStar 500 airliner over runway .... 2·00 2·50
501/4 .... Set of 4 5·25 4·50

(Des A. Theobald (£1), C. Abbott (others). Litho Questa)

1985 (7 June). *Life and Times of Queen Elizabeth the Queen Mother.* T **148** *and similar vert designs. Multicoloured.* W w **16**. P 14½ × 14.
505 7p. Attending reception at Lancaster House 25 20
506 22p. With Prince Charles, Mark Phillips and Princess Anne at Falklands Memorial Service 60 50
       w. Wmk inverted .... 14·00
507 27p. Type **148** 70 60
508 54p. With Prince Henry at his christening (from photo by Lord Snowdon) .. 1·25 1·25
505/8 .... Set of 4 2·50 2·25
MS509 91×73 mm £1 With Princess Diana at Trooping the Colour. Wmk sideways .. 2·50 2·25

149 Captain J. McBride and H.M.S. *Jason*, 1765

149a Philibert Commerson and Commerson's Dolphin

(Des O. Bell. Litho Questa)

1985 (30 Sept). *Early Cartographers.* T **149** *and similar horiz designs. Multicoloured.* W w **14** (*sideways*). P 14 × 14½.
510 7p. Type **149** .... 1·10 40
511 22p. Commodore J. Byron and H.M.S. *Dolphin and Tamar*, 1765 .. 1·60 80
512 27p. Vice-Admiral R. FitzRoy and H.M.S. *Beagle*, 1831 ...... 1·75 85
513 54p. Admiral Sir B. J. Sullivan and H.M.S. *Philomel*, 1842 .... 2·50 1·75
510/13 .... Set of 4 6·25 3·50

(Des I. Strange. Litho Questa)

1985 (4 Nov). *Early Naturalists.* T **149a** *and similar vert designs. Multicoloured.* W w **14**. P 14½×14.
514 7p. Type **149a** .... 1·00 40
515 22p. René Primevère Lesson and *Lessonia sp.* (kelp) .... 1·50 1·10
516 27p. Joseph Paul Gaimard and Common Diving Petrel .... 2·25 1·90
517 54p. Charles Darwin and *Calceolaria darwinii* .... 2·50 2·75
514/17 .... Set of 4 6·50 5·50

MINIMUM PRICE

The minimum price quote is 10p which represents a handling charge rather than a basis for valuing common stamps. For further notes about prices see introductory pages.

1986   Falkland Islands — 17

150 Painted Keyhole Limpet (*Fissurella picta*)
150a Princesses Elizabeth and Margaret, 1932
153 Prince Andrew and Miss Sarah Ferguson presenting Polo Trophy, Windsor
154 Survey Party, Sapper Hill

(Des I. Strange. Litho Questa)

1986 (10 Feb). *Seashells. T* **150** *and similar horiz designs. Multicoloured. W* **16** (*sideways*). *P* 14×14½.

518	7p. Type **150**		85	60
519	22p. *Provocator palliata* (*Odontocymbiola magellanica*)		1·50	1·40
520	27p. Patagonian or Falkland Scallop (*Chlamys lischkei*)		1·75	2·25
521	54p. Rough Thorn Drupe (*Acanthina monodon imbricata*)		2·75	3·50
518/21		Set of 4	6·25	7·00

(Des A. Theobald. Litho Format)

1986 (21 Apr). *60th Birthday of Queen Elizabeth II. T* **150a** *and similar vert designs. Multicoloured. W* **16** *P* 14×14½.

522	10p. Type **150a**		20	25
523	24p. Queen making Christmas television broadcast, 1958		35	50
524	29p. In robes of Order of the Thistle, St. Giles Cathedral, Edinburgh, 1962		35	60
525	45p. Aboard Royal Yacht *Britannia*, U.S.A., 1976		1·25	1·25
526	58p. At Crown Agents Head Office, London, 1983		80	1·50
522/6		Set of 5	2·75	3·50

(Des D. Miller. Litho Questa)

1986 (10 Nov). *Royal Wedding. T* **153** *and similar vert designs. Multicoloured. W* **16**. *P* 14½×14.

536	17p. Type **153**		85	50
537	22p. Prince Andrew and Duchess of York on wedding day		95	65
538	29p. Prince Andrew in battledress at opening of Fox Bay Mill		1·25	90
536/8		Set of 3	2·75	1·90

(Des L. Curtis. Litho Questa)

1987 (9 Feb). *Bicentenary of Royal Engineers' Royal Warrant. T* **154** *and similar horiz designs. Multicoloured. W* w **16** (*sideways*). *P* 14×14½.

539	10p. Type **154**		1·25	80
540	24p. Mine clearance by robot		1·75	1·50
541	29p. Boxer Bridge, Stanley		2·00	2·50
542	58p. Unloading mail, Mount Pleasant Airport		2·75	4·00
539/42		Set of 4	7·00	8·00

151 S.S. *Great Britain* crossing Atlantic, 1845
152 Head of Rockhopper Penguin
155 Southern Sea Lion
156 *Suillus luteus*

(Des O. Bell. Litho Format)

1986 (22 May). *"Ameripex '86" International Stamp Exhibition, Chicago. Centenary of Arrival of S.S. "Great Britain" in Falkland Islands. T* **151** *and similar horiz designs. Multicoloured. W* w **16** (*sideways**). *P* 14.

527	10p. Type **151**		50	60
528	24p. Beached at Sparrow Cove, 1937		60	80
529	29p. Refloated on pontoon, 1970		70	90
530	58p. Undergoing restoration, Bristol, 1986 w. Wmk Crown to right of CA		80	2·25
			70·00	
527/30		Set of 4	2·40	4·00
MS531	109×109 mm. Nos. 527/30. Wmk upright		2·00	3·25

The normal sideways watermark shows Crown to left of CA as seen from the back of the stamp.

(Des I. Strange. Litho Questa)

1986 (25 Aug). *Rockhopper Penguins. T* **152** *and similar vert designs. Multicoloured. W* w **16**. *P* 14½×14.

532	10p. Type **152**		1·00	70
533	24p. Rockhopper Penguins at sea		1·75	1·75
534	29p. Courtship display		2·00	2·00
535	58p. Adult with chick		2·50	4·50
532/5		Set of 4	6·50	8·00

(Des I. Strange. Litho Questa)

1987 (27 Apr). *Seals. T* **155** *and similar horiz designs. Multicoloured. W* w **16** (*sideways*). *P* 14½.

543	10p. Type **155**		85	55
544	24p. Falkland Fur Seal		1·75	90
545	29p. Southern Elephant Seal		1·90	1·50
546	58p. Leopard Seal		2·75	3·00
543/6		Set of 4	6·50	5·50

(Des I. Strange. Litho Questa)

1987 (14 Sept). *Fungi. T* **156** *and similar vert designs. Multicoloured. W* w **16** *P* 14½×14.

547	10p. Type **156**		1·75	85
548	24p. *Mycena* sp.		2·75	2·00
549	29p. *Hygrophorous adonis* ("*Camarophyllus adonis*")		3·00	3·00
550	58p. *Gerronema schusteri*		4·50	5·00
547/50		Set of 4	11·00	9·75

NEW INFORMATION

The editor is always interested to correspond with people who have new information that will improve or correct the Catalogue.

18 — Falkland Islands 1987

157 Victoria Cottage Home, c 1912

158 Morris Truck, Fitzroy, 1940

(Des D. Hartley. Litho Questa)

1987 (8 Dec). *Local Hospitals.* T **157** *and similar horiz designs. Multicoloured. W w* **16** *(sideways). P* 14.
551	10p. Type **157** ..		50	25
552	24p. King Edward VII Memorial Hospital, c 1914		85	55
553	29p. Churchill Wing, King Edward VII Memorial Hospital, c 1953		95	60
554	58p. Prince Andrew Wing, New Hospital, 1987		1·50	1·25
551/4	.. ..	Set of 4	3·50	2·40

(Des D. Hartley. Litho Questa)

1988 (11 Apr). *Early Vehicles.* T **158** *and similar horiz designs. Multicoloured. W w* **16** *(sideways). P* 14.
555	10p. Type **158**		50	25
556	24p. Citroen "Kegresse" half-track, San Carlos, 1929		85	55
557	29p. Ford one ton truck, Port Stanley, 1933		95	60
558	58p. Ford "Model T" car, Darwin, 1935		1·50	1·25
555/8	.. ..	Set of 4	3·50	2·40

159 Kelp Goose

(Des I. Strange. Litho Walsall)

1988 (25 July). *Falkland Islands Geese.* T **159** *and similar horiz designs. Multicoloured. W w* **16** *(sideways). P* 13½×14.
559	10p. Type **159**		2·00	55
560	24p. Magellan ("Upland") Goose ..		2·75	70
561	29p. Ruddy-headed Goose ..		3·00	90
562	58p. Ashy-headed Goose ..		4·50	2·00
559/62	.. ..	Set of 4	11·00	3·75

159a Silver from Lloyd's Nelson Collection

(Des D. Miller (10p., 24p.), E. Nisbet and D. Miller (29p., 58p.). Litho Format)

1988 (14 Nov). *300th Anniv of Lloyd's of London.* T **159**a *and similar multicoloured designs. W w* **14** *(sideways on 24p., 29p.). P* 14.
563	10p. Type **159**a		40	30
564	24p. Falkland Islands hydroponic market garden (*horiz*)		75	65
565	29p. A.E.S. (mail ship) (*horiz*) ..		1·25	75
566	58p. *Charles Cooper* (full-rigged ship), 1866		1·50	1·25
	w. Wmk inverted		28·00	
563/6		Set of 4	3·50	2·75

160 *Padua* (barque)

(Des A. Theobald. Litho Questa)

1989 (28 Feb)–**90**. *Cape Horn Sailing Ships.* T **160** *and similar multicoloured designs. W w* **14** *(sideways on horiz designs). P* 14.
567	1p. Type **160**		80	60
568	2p. *Priwall* (barque) (*vert*) ..		1·50	1·25
569	3p. *Passat* (barque) ..		1·50	1·25
570	4p. *Archibald Russell* (barque) (*vert*)		1·00	80
571	5p. *Pamir* (barque) (*vert*) ..		1·00	80
572	6p. *Mozart* (barquentine) ..		1·75	1·25
573	7p. *Pommern* (barque) ..		1·25	1·00
574	8p. *Preussen* (full-rigged ship)		1·25	1·00
575	9p. *Fennia* (barque) ..		1·75	1·25
576	10p. *Cassard* (barque) ..		1·25	1·00
577	20p. *Lawhill* (barque) ..		2·00	2·00
578	25p. *Garthpool* (barque) ..		2·00	2·00
579	50p. *Grace Harwar* (full-rigged ship)		3·00	3·00
580	£1 *Criccieth Castle* (full-rigged ship)		7·50	7·50
581	£3 *Cutty Sark* (full-rigged ship) (*vert*)		9·00	8·50
582	£5 *Flying Cloud* (full-rigged ship) (2.1.90)		11·00	9·00
567/82		Set of 16	42·00	38·00

For 2, 3, 6, 9p. and £1 values watermarked w **16** and with imprint dates see Nos. 613/25.

161 Southern Right Whale

(Des I. Strange. Litho Questa)

1989 (15 May). *Baleen Whales.* T **161** *and similar horiz designs. Multicoloured. W w* **16** *(sideways). P* 13½×14.
583	10p. Type **161**		1·25	40
584	24p. Minke Whale		2·00	85
585	29p. Humpback Whale ..		2·25	1·25
586	58p. Blue Whale		3·50	2·50
583/6	.. ..	Set of 4	8·00	4·50

MINIMUM PRICE

The minimum price quote is 10p which represents a handling charge rather than a basis for valuing common stamps. For further notes about prices see introductory pages.

1989   Falkland Islands — 19

162 "Gymkhana" (Sarah Gilding)

163 Vice-Admiral Sturdee and H.M.S. *Invincible* (battle cruiser)

165a Queen Mother in Dover

165b On Bridge of Queen Elizabeth (liner), 1946

(Adapted G. Vasarhelyi. Litho Walsall)

1989 (16 Sept). *Sports Associations' Activities.* T **162** and similar horiz designs showing children's drawings. Multicoloured. W w **16** (*sideways*). P 14.

587	5p. Type **162**	..	20	20
588	10p. "Steer Riding" (Karen Steen) ..		30	30
589	17p. "Sheep Shearing" (Colin Shepherd)		45	45
590	24p. "Sheepdog Trials" (Rebecca Edwards)		60	70
591	29p. "Horse Racing" (Dilys Blackley)	..	70	80
592	45p. "Sack Race" (Donna Newell)	..	1·00	1·10
587/92	.. .. Set of 6		3·00	3·25

(Des D. Miller. Litho Questa)

1990 (4 Aug). *90th Birthday of Queen Elizabeth the Queen Mother.* W w **16**. P 14×15 (26p.) or 14½ (£1).

606	**165**a	26p. multicoloured	1·00	65
607	**165**b	£1 brownish black & dp carmine-red	2·75	2·75

(Des C. Collins. Litho B.D.T.)

1989 (8 Dec). *75th Anniv of Battle of the Falkland Islands and 50th Anniv of Battle of the River Plate.* T **163** and similar vert designs. Multicoloured. W w **16**. P 13½.

593	10p. Type **163**	40	30
594	24p. Vice-Admiral Graf von Spee and *Scharnhorst* (German cruiser) ..	80	75
595	29p. Commodore Harwood and H.M.S. *Ajax* (cruiser) ..	90	85
596	58p. Captain Langsdorff and *Admiral Graf Spee* (German pocket battleship) ..	1·75	2·00
593/6	.. .. .. Set of 4	3·50	3·50

166 Black-browed Albatrosses

167 *Gavilea australis*

(Des I. Strange. Litho Questa)

1990 (3 Oct). *Black-browed Albatross.* T **166** and similar vert designs. Multicoloured. W w **16**. P 13½×14.

608	12p. Type **166**	75	50
609	26p. Female with egg	1·40	1·00
610	31p. Adult and chick	1·60	1·25
611	62p. Black-browed Albatross in flight ..	2·75	3·00
608/11	.. .. .. Set of 4	6·00	5·25

164 Southern Sea Lions on Kidney Island

165 Supermarine Spitfire Mk 1 *Falkland Islands I*

(Des I. Strange. Litho Questa)

1990 (9 Apr). *Nature Reserves and Sanctuaries.* T **164** and similar vert designs. Multicoloured. W w **16**. P 14½.

597	12p. Type **164**	60	35
598	26p. Black-browed Albatrosses on Beauchene Island	1·40	70
599	31p. Penguin colony on Bird Island	1·40	90
600	62p. Tussock grass on Elephant Jason Island	1·50	1·75
597/600	.. .. .. Set of 4	4·50	3·25

1991 (7 Jan). *As Nos.* 568/9, 572, 575 *and* 580, *but* W w **16** (*sideways on horiz designs*) *and with* "1991" *imprint date added at foot.* P 14.

613	2p. *Priwall* (barque) (*vert*) ..	60	80
614	3p. *Passat* (barque)	60	80
617	6p. *Mozart* (barquentine) ..	70	80
620	9p. *Fennia* (barque)	80	90
625	£1 *Criccieth Castle* (full-rigged ship)	2·75	3·50
613/25	.. .. .. Set of 5	5·00	6·00

(Des A. Theobald. Litho B.D.T.)

1990 (3 May). *"Stamp World London 90" International Stamp Exhibition, London. Presentation Spitfires.* T **165** and similar horiz designs. Multicoloured. W w **14** (*sideways*). P 14.

601	12p. Type **165**	65	35
602	26p. Supermarine Spitfire Mk 1 *Falkland Islands VII*	1·25	70
603	31p. Cockpit and wing of *Falkland Islands I*	1·25	1·00
604	62p. Squadron scramble, 1940 ..	1·75	2·00
601/4	.. .. .. Set of 4	4·50	3·50
MS605	114×100 mm. £1 Supermarine Spitfire Mk 1 in action, 1940 ..	4·00	2·50

For No. **MS**605 with additional inscription see No. **MS**628.

(Des A. Theobald. Litho B.D.T.)

1991 (18 Mar). *Second Visit of H.R.H. The Duke of Edinburgh.* As No. **MS**605, *but with Exhibition emblem replaced by* "SECOND VISIT OF HRH THE DUKE OF EDINBURGH". W w **16** (*sideways*). P 14.

MS628   114×100 mm. £1 Spitfire Mk. I in action, 1940   5·50   7·00

The margin of No. **MS**628 also shows the Exhibition emblem omitted and has the same commemorative inscription added.

(Des I. Strange. Litho Questa)

1991 (18 Mar). *Orchids.* T **167** and similar vert designs. Multicoloured. W w **14**. P 14×13½.

629	12p. Type **167**	75	70
630	26p. Dog Orchid	1·25	1·00
631	31p. *Chloraea gaudichaudii* ..	1·40	1·50
632	62p. Yellow Orchid	2·50	3·75
629/32	.. .. .. Set of 4	5·50	6·25

20 — Falkland Islands   1991

168 Heads of Two King Penguins

169 ½d and 2½d Stamps of September 1891

(Des I. Strange. Litho Questa)

1991 (26 Aug). *Endangered Species. King Penguin. T* **168** *and similar vert designs. Multicoloured. W w* **16**. *P* 14.

633	2p. Type **168**	.. .. ..	70	70
634	6p. Female incubating egg		90	90
635	12p. Female with two chicks	..	1·25	1·00
636	20p. Penguin underwater ..		1·50	1·25
637	31p. Parents feeding their chick	..	1·60	1·90
638	62p. Courtship dance	..	2·25	2·75
633/8		Set of 6	7·50	7·75

Nos. 637/8 do not include the W.W.F. panda emblem.

(Des D. Miller. Litho Questa)

1991 (10 Sept). *Centenary of Bisected Surcharges. T* **169** *and similar horiz designs. Multicoloured. W w* **16** *(sideways). P* 14½.

639	12p. Type **169**	.. ..	60	50
640	26p. Cover of March 1891 franked with strip of five ½d bisects		1·00	1·00
641	31p. Unsevered pair of ½d. surcharge	..	1·25	1·50
642	62p. *Isis* (mail ship)	..	2·00	3·25
639/42		Set of 4	4·25	5·50

169*a* Map of Re-enactment Voyages and *Eye of the Wind* (cadet brig)

(Des R. Watton. Litho Walsall)

1991 (12 Dec). *500th Anniv of Discovery of America by Columbus and Re-enactment Voyages. T* **169***a* *and similar horiz designs. Multicoloured. W w* **14** *(sideways). P* 13½×14.

643	14p. Type **169***a* ..	..		60	50
644	29p. Compass rose and *Soren Larsen* (cadet brigantine)	..	1·25	1·40
645	34p. *Santa Maria, Pinta* and *Nina*	..	1·50	1·75
646	68p. Columbus and *Santa Maria*	..	2·50	4·00
643/6		Set of 4	5·25	7·00

169*b* "Stanley Through The Narrows" (A. Asprey)

(Des D. Miller. Litho Questa (68p.), Walsall (others))

1992 (6 Feb). *40th Anniv of Queen Elizabeth II's Accession. T* **169***b* *and similar horiz designs. Multicoloured. W w* **14** *(sideways). P* 14.

647	7p. Type **169***b*	.. ..	45	35
648	14p. "Hill Cove" (A. Asprey)	..	70	60
649	29p. "San Carlos Water" (A. Asprey)	..	1·10	95
650	34p. Three portraits of Queen Elizabeth	1·25	1·25
651	68p. Queen Elizabeth II	..	1·75	2·00
647/51		Set of 5	4·75	4·75

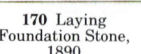

170 Laying Foundation Stone, 1890

170*a* San Carlos Cemetery

(Des N. Shewring. Litho Questa)

1992 (21 Feb). *Centenary of Christ Church Cathedral, Stanley. T* **170** *and similar multicoloured designs. W w* **14** *(sideways on 68p.). P* 14½.

652	14p. Type **170**	.. ..	75	55
653	29p. Interior of Cathedral, 1920	..	1·40	1·00
654	34p. Bishop's chair	..	1·60	1·25
655	68p. Cathedral in 1900 (*horiz*)	..	2·00	1·90
652/5		Set of 4	5·25	4·25

(Des N. Shewring. Litho Questa)

1992 (14 June). *10th Anniv of Liberation. T* **170***a* *and similar square designs. Multicoloured. W w* **14** *(sideways). P* 14.

656	14p. + 6p. Type **170***a*	..	75	1·25
657	29p. + 11p. War Memorial, Port Stanley	1·40	1·75
658	34p. + 16p. South Atlantic medal	..	1·60	1·90
659	68p. + 32p. Government House, Port Stanley	..	2·75	3·00
656/9		Set of 4	6·00	7·00
MS660	115×115 mm. Nos. 656/9		6·00	7·00

The premiums on Nos. 656/60 were for the S.S.A.F.A.

171 Captain John Davis and Backstaff

(Des R. Watton. Litho Questa)

1992 (14 Aug). *400th Anniv of First Sighting of the Falkland Islands. T* **171** *and similar horiz designs. Multicoloured. W w* **14** *(sideways). P* 14½.

661	22p. Type **171**	.. ..	1·25	80
662	29p. Capt. John Davis	..	1·50	1·10
663	34p. Queen Elizabeth I and Queen Elizabeth II		1·75	1·50
664	68p. *Desire* sighting Falkland Islands	2·75	3·00
661/4		Set of 4	6·50	5·75

NEW INFORMATION

The editor is always interested to correspond with people who have new information that will improve or correct the Catalogue.

1992   Falkland Islands — 21

172 Private, Falkland Islands Volunteers, 1892

173 South American Tern

(Des C. Collins. Litho Questa)

1992 (1 Oct). *Centenary of Falkland Islands Defence Force and 50th Anniv of Affiliation to West Yorkshire Regiment.* T **172** *and similar vert designs. Multicoloured.* W w **14**. P 14.

665	7p. Type **172**	..	..	..	45	30
666	14p. Officer, Falkland Islands Defence Corps, 1914				70	50
667	22p. Officer, Falkland Islands Defence Force, 1920				90	70
668	29p. Private, Falkland Islands Defence Force, 1939–45				1·10	90
669	34p. Officer, West Yorkshire Regiment, 1942				1·40	1·25
670	68p. Private, West Yorkshire Regiment, 1942				2·40	2·10
665/70		..	..	Set of 6	6·25	5·25

(Des I. Strange. Litho Questa)

1993 (2 Jan). *Gulls and Terns.* T **173** *and similar horiz designs. Multicoloured.* W w **16** (*sideways*). P 14×14½.

671	15p. Type **173**				85	75
672	31p. Brown-hooded Gull ("Pink breasted Gull")				1·40	1·25
673	36p. Magellan Gull				1·60	1·75
674	72p. Southern Black-backed Gull ("Dominican Gull")				2·75	4·00
671/4		..	..	Set of 4	6·00	7·00

174 Queen Elizabeth 2

(Des N. Shewring. Litho Questa)

1993 (22 Jan). *Visit of the* Queen Elizabeth 2 (*cruise liner*). *Sheet* 60×42 *mm.* W w **14** (*sideways*). P 14.
MS675 174 £2 multicoloured .. .. 5·25 5·50

174a Avro Vulcan B.1A

(Des A. Theobald. Litho Questa)

1993 (1 Apr). *75th Anniv of Royal Air Force.* T **174a** *and similar horiz designs. Multicoloured.* W w **14** (*sideways**). P 14.

676	15p. Type **174a**	..	..	..	65	85
677	15p. Lockheed C-130K Hercules		..		65	85
678	15p. Boeing-Vertol CH-47 Chinook		..		65	85
679	15p. Lockheed L-1011 TriStar 500				65	85
676/9				Set of 4	2·40	3·00

MS680 110×77 mm. 36p. Hawker Siddeley Andover CC.2; 36p. Westland Wessex HC-2 helicopter; 36p. Panavia Tornado F Mk 3; 36p. McDonnell Douglas F-4M Phantom II .. 3·75 4·75

w. Wmk Crown to right of CA

*The normal sideways watermark shows Crown to left of CA, as seen from the back of the stamp.

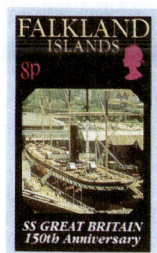

175 Short-finned Squid

176 *Great Britain* in Dry Dock, Bristol

(Des O. Ball. Litho Questa)

1993 (1 July). *Fisheries.* T **175** *and similar horiz designs. Multicoloured.* W w **16** (*sideways*). P 14.

681	15p. Type **175**			..	60	60
682	31p. Catch of Whip-tailed Hake		..	..	1·25	1·40
683	36p. *Falklands Protector* (fisheries patrol vessel)				1·50	1·75
684	72p. Britten Norman Islander patrol aircraft and *Pomorze* (fish factory ship)				2·25	4·00
681/4		..	..	Set of 4	5·00	7·00

(Des O. Ball. Litho Questa)

1993 (19 July). *150th Anniv of Launch of* Great Britain (*liner*). T **176** *and similar vert design. Multicoloured.* W w **16**. P 14×13½.

685	8p. Type **176**	..	..	..	50	50
686	£1 *Great Britain* at sea	..		..	2·75	4·00

177 *Explorer* (liner)

178 Pony

(Des N. Shewring. Litho Questa)

1993 (1 Oct). *Tourism.* T **177** *and similar horiz designs. Multicoloured.* W w **14** (*sideways*). P 14.

687	16p. Type **177**	..	..	..	75	60
688	34p. Rockhopper Penguins				1·50	1·25
689	39p. *World Discoverer* (liner)		..		1·75	1·75
690	78p. *Columbus Caravelle* (liner)				2·25	2·75
687/90		..	..	Set of 4	5·50	5·75

(Des E. Tenney. Litho Walsall)

1993 (1 Dec). *Pets.* T **178** *and similar multicoloured designs.* W w **16** (*sideways on* 8p., 16p., 34p.; *inverted on* 39p.). P 14×14½ (*horiz*) *or* 14½×14 (*vert*).

691	8p. Type **178**	..	..	..	60	60
692	16p. Lamb	..	..	..	..	75	75
693	34p. Puppy and cat		..	..	1·75	1·75

22 — Falkland Islands 1993

694	39p. Kitten (*vert*)	..	..	2·00	2·00
695	78p. Collie dog (*vert*)	..	..	2·75	4·00
691/5			Set of 5	7·00	8·25

(178*a*)

1994 (18 Feb). *"Hong Kong '94" International Stamp Exhibition*. Nos. 691/5 additionally inscribed with the exhibition logo as T **178a**.

696	8p. Type **178**	..	..	50	60
697	16p. Lamb	..	..	65	75
698	34p. Puppy and cat	..	..	1·50	1·75
699	39p. Kitten (*vert*)	..	..	1·60	2·00
700	78p. Collie dog (*vert*)	..	..	2·50	4·00
696/700			Set of 5	6·00	8·25

On the vertical designs "FALKLAND ISLANDS" ranges left instead of being centred as on Nos. 694/5.

179 Goose Barnacles

180 Dockyard Blacksmith's Shop and Sir James Clark Ross (explorer)

(Des T. Chater. Litho Walsall)

1994 (4 Apr). *Inshore Marine Life*. T **179** and similar multicoloured designs. W w **16** (*sideways on horiz designs*). P 14.

701	1p. Type **179**	..	..	40	50
702	2p. Painted Shrimp (*horiz*)			50	50
703	8p. Patagonian Copper Limpet (*horiz*)		..	75	75
704	9p. Eleginops ("Mullet") (*horiz*)	..		75	75
705	10p. Sea Anemones (*horiz*)			75	60
706	20p. Flathead Eelpout (*horiz*)		..	1·25	90
707	25p. Spider Crab (*horiz*)	..		1·25	90
708	50p. Lobster Krill ..	..	..	2·25	2·00
709	80p. Falkland Skate (*horiz*)			2·50	2·50
710	£1 Centollón Crab (*horiz*)			2·50	2·50
711	£3 Wilton's Nototen ("Rock Cod") (*horiz*)			7·50	6·25
712	£5 Octopus	..	..	11·00	10·50
701/12			Set of 12	28·00	26·00

A similar 5p. value, showing a smelt and incorrectly inscribed "Austro Menidia Smithii", was withdrawn before issue.

For miniature sheet containing £1, wmk w **14** and with imprint date, see No. **MS**784.

(Des J. Peck. Litho Questa)

1994 (1 July). *150th Anniv of Founding of Stanley*. T **180** and similar horiz designs. Multicoloured. W w **14** (*sideways*). P 14.

713	9p. Type **180**	..	..	50	50
714	17p. 21 Fitzroy Road (home of Chaplain James Moody)			75	60
715	30p. Stanley Cottage (built by Dr. Henry Hamblin)			1·25	1·25
716	35p. Pioneer Row and Sgt-maj Henry Felton			1·50	1·75
717	40p. Government House (designed by Governor R. Moody)		..	1·60	1·90
718	65p. View of Stanley and Edward Stanley, Earl of Derby (Secretary of State for the Colonies) ..			2·25	3·00
713/18			Set of 6	7·00	8·00

181 Lockheed L-1011 TriStar over Gypsy Cove

(Des J. Peck. Litho Walsall)

1994 (24 Oct). *Falkland Beaches*. T **181** and similar horiz designs. Multicoloured. W w **16** (*sideways*). P 14.

719	17p. Type **181**	..	..	85	70
720	35p. *Explorer* (liner) off Sea Lion Island		..	1·60	1·40
721	40p. Britten Norman Islander aircraft at Pebble Island		..	2·00	2·00
722	65p. Landrover at Volunteer Beach			2·25	3·50
719/22			Set of 4	6·00	7·00

182 Mission House, Keppel Island

183 *Lupinus arboreus*

(Des G. Vasarhelyi. Litho Questa)

1994 (1 Dec). *150th Anniv of South American Missionary Society*. T **182** and similar horiz designs. Multicoloured. W w **16** (*sideways*). P 14.

723	5p. Type **182**	..	..	35	40
724	17p. Thomas Bridges (compiler of Yaghan dictionary)			65	65
725	40p. Fuegian Indians	..	..	1·40	1·75
726	65p. Capt. Allen Gardiner and *Allen Gardiner* (schooner)			1·75	2·50
723/6			Set of 4	3·75	4·75

(Des I. Strange. Litho Questa)

1995 (3 Jan). *Flowering Shrubs*. T **183** and similar vert designs. Multicoloured. W w **16**. P 14½ × 14.

727	9p. Type **183**	..	..	50	50
728	17p. *Hebe elliptica*	..	..	70	70
729	30p. *Fuschia magellanica*	..		95	95
730	35p. *Berberis ilicifolia*	..	..	1·10	1·10
731	40p. *Ulex europaeus*	..	..	1·25	1·25
732	65p. *Hebe x franciscana*	..		2·00	2·75
727/32			Set of 6	6·00	6·50

184 Magellanic Oystercatcher

(Des I. Strange. Litho B.D.T.)

1995 (1 Mar). *Shore Birds*. T **184** and similar horiz designs. Multicoloured. W w **16** (*sideways*). P 13½.

733	17p. Type **184**	..	..	1·00	70
734	35p. Rufous-chested Dotterel		..	1·60	1·40
735	40p. Blackish Oystercatcher		..	1·75	1·75
736	65p. Two-banded Plover	..	..	3·00	4·00
733/6			Set of 4	6·50	7·00

1995 Falkland Islands — 23

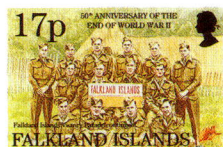

184a Falkland Islands Contingent in Victory Parade

(Des R. Watton. Litho Questa)

1995 (8 May). *50th Anniv of End of Second World War.* T **184a** *and similar multicoloured designs.* W w **14** (*sideways*). P 14.
737	17p. Type **184a**	..	75	75
738	35p. Governor Sir Alan Cardinall on Bren gun-carrier	..	1·40	1·40
739	40p. H.M.A.S. *Esperance Bay* (troopship)		1·50	1·75
740	65p. H.M.S. *Exeter* (cruiser)	..	2·75	3·75
737/40	.. .. ..	Set of 4	5·75	7·00
MS741	75×85 mm. £1 Reverse of 1939–45 War Medal (*vert*). Wmk upright	..	2·50	3·50

185 Ox and Cart

186 Kelp Geese

(Des N. Shewring. Litho B.D.T.)

1995 (1 Aug). *Transporting Peat.* T **185** *and similar horiz designs. Multicoloured.* W w **16** (*sideways*). P 14.
742	17p. Type **185**	..	60	50
743	35p. Horse and cart	..	1·10	1·10
744	40p. Caterpillar tractor pulling sleigh	..	1·25	1·25
745	65p. Lorry	..	2·25	3·00
742/5	.. .. ..	Set of 4	4·75	5·25

(Des Sonia Felton. Litho B.D.T.)

1995 (11 Sept). *Wildlife.* T **186** *and similar vert designs. Multicoloured.* W w **16**. P 13½.
746	35p. Type **186**	..	1·10	1·10
	a. Sheetlet. Nos. 746/51	..	5·75	
747	35p. Black-browed Albatross	..	1·10	1·10
748	35p. Blue-eyed Cormorants	..	1·10	1·10
749	35p. Magellanic Penguins	..	1·10	1·10
750	35p. Fur Seals	..	1·10	1·10
751	35p. Rockhopper Penguins	..	1·10	1·10
746/51	.. ..	Set of 6	5·75	5·75

Nos. 746/51 were printed together, *se-tenant*, in sheetlets of 6, with the backgrounds forming a composite design.

187 Cottontail Rabbit

(Des A. Robinson. Litho Walsall)

1995 (6 Nov). *Introduced Wild Animals.* T **187** *and similar horiz designs. Multicoloured.* W w **14** (*sideways*). P 14.
752	9p. Type **187**	..	65	65
753	17p. Brown Hare	..	90	75
754	35p. Guanacos	..	1·40	1·25
755	40p. Fox	..	1·60	1·40
756	65p. Otter ..	..	2·50	2·50
752/6	.. ..	Set of 5	6·25	5·50

188 Princess Anne and Government House

(Des D. Miller. Litho Walsall)

1996 (30 Jan). *Royal Visit.* T **188** *and similar horiz designs. Multicoloured.* W w **14** (*sideways*). P 14½×14.
757	9p. Type **188**	..	45	45
758	19p. Falklands War Memorial, San Carlos Cemetery	..	75	65
759	30p. Christ Church Cathedral	..	1·10	1·10
760	73p. Helicopter over Goose Green	..	2·50	3·00
757/60	.. ..	Set of 4	4·25	4·75

188a Queen Elizabeth II and Steeple Jason

(Des D. Miller. Litho B.D.T.)

1996 (21 Apr). *70th Birthday of Queen Elizabeth II.* T **188a** *and similar vert designs, each incorporating a different photograph of the Queen.* W w **14**. P 13½.
761	17p. Type **188a**	..	60	50
762	40p. *Tamar* (container ship)	..	1·50	1·25
763	45p. New Island	..	1·50	1·40
764	65p. Falkland Islands Community School	..	1·60	1·60
761/4	.. ..	Set of 4	4·75	4·25
MS765	64×66 mm. £1 Queen Elizabeth II	..	2·40	3·00

189 Mounted Postman, *c.* 1890

(Des A. Theobald. Litho Walsall)

1996 (8 June). *"CAPEX '96" International Stamp Exhibition, Toronto. Mail Transport.* T **189** *and similar horiz designs. Multicoloured.* W w **16** (*sideways*). P 14.
766	9p. Type **189**	..	75	60
767	40p. Noorduyn Norseman V seaplane	..	1·75	1·50
768	45p. *Forrest* (freighter) at San Carlos	..	1·75	1·60

769	76p. De Havilland D.H.C.2 Beaver seaplane			2·75	2·75
766/9			Set of 4	6·25	5·75
MS770	110×80 mm. £1 L.M.S. Class "Jubilee" steam locomotive No. 5606 *Falkland Islands* (47×31 *mm*). P 13½×14			2·40	3·25

190 Southern Bottlenose Whale

(Des E. King. Litho Walsall)

1996 (2 Sept). *Beaked Whales. T* **190** *and similar horiz designs. Multicoloured. W* w **14** (*sideways*). *P* 13½×14.

771	9p. Type **190**		45	45
772	30p. Cuvier's Beaked Whale		1·10	1·10
773	35p. Straptoothed Beaked Whale		1·25	1·25
774	75p. Gray's Beaked Whale		2·40	2·40
771/4		Set of 4	4·75	4·75

191 Magellanic Penguins performing Courtship Dance

(Des I. Strange. Litho Walsall)

1997 (2 Jan). *Magellanic Penguins. T* **191** *and similar horiz designs. Multicoloured. W* w **14** (*sideways*). *P* 14½.

775	17p. Type **191**		65	55
776	35p. Penguin in burrow		1·25	1·00
777	40p. Adult and chick		1·40	1·25
778	65p. Group of Penguins swimming		1·75	1·75
775/8		Set of 4	4·50	4·00

192 Black Pejerry 193 Coral Fern

(Des T. Chater and D. Miller. Litho Questa)

1997 (3 Feb). *"HONG KONG '97" International Stamp Exhibition. Sheet* 130×90 *mm. W* w **14** (*sideways*). *P* 14.
MS779 **192** £1 multicoloured .. .. 2·50 2·50

(Des I. Strange. Litho Walsall)

1997 (3 Mar). *Ferns. T* **193** *and similar vert designs. Multicoloured. W* w **14**. *P* 14½.

780	17p. Type **193**		70	45
781	35p. Adder's Tongue Fern		1·25	1·00
782	40p. Fuegian Tall Fern		1·40	1·10
783	65p. Small Fern		1·75	1·75
780/3		Set of 4	4·50	3·75

(Des T. Chater. Litho Walsall)

1997 (20 June). *Return of Hong Kong to China. Sheet* 130×90 *mm, containing design as No.* 710. *With imprint date. W* w **14** (*sideways*). *P* 14.
MS784 £1 Centollón Crab .. .. 2·50 2·50

193a Queen Elizabeth holding Bouquet, 1993

(Des N. Shewring (No. **MS**791), D. Miller (others). Litho Questa)

1997 (10 July). *Golden Wedding of Queen Elizabeth and Prince Philip. T* **193**a *amd similar multicoloured designs. W* w **16**. *P* 14½.

785	9p. Type **193**a		50	40
	a. Horiz pair. Nos. 785/6		1·00	80
786	9p. Prince Philip and horse, 1985		50	40
787	17p. Queen Elizabeth in phaeton at Trooping the Colour, 1996		80	65
	a. Horiz pair. Nos. 787/8		1·60	1·25
788	17p. Prince Philip in R.A.F. uniform		80	65
789	40p. Queen Elizabeth wearing red coat, 1986		1·00	1·00
	a. Horiz pair. Nos. 789/90		2·00	2·00
790	40p. Prince William and Princess Beatrice on horseback		1·00	1·00
785/90		Set of 6	4·25	3·50
MS791	110×71 mm. £1.50, Queen Elizabeth and Prince Philip in landau (*horiz*). W w **14** (*sideways*). P 14×14½		3·50	3·50

Nos. 785/6, 787/8 and 789/90 were each printed together, *se-tenant*, in horizontal pairs throughout the sheets with the backgrounds forming composite designs.

194 Bull Point Lighthouse

(Des J. Peck. Litho Walsall)

1997 (4 Aug*). *Lighthouses. T* **194** *and similar horiz designs. Multicoloured. W* w **14** (*sideways*). *P* 14.

792	9p. Type **194**		60	40
793	30p. Cape Pembroke Lighthouse		1·25	1·25
794	£1 Cape Meredith Lighthouse		2·75	3·00
792/4		Set of 3	4·25	4·25

*This is the local date of issue. The Crown Agents released the stamps in London on 4 July.

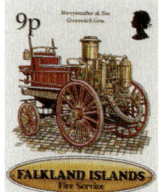

195 Forster's Caracara   196 Merryweather and Son Greenwich Gem Fire Engine

1997   **Falkland Islands — 25**

(Des Sonia Felton. Litho Questa)

1997 (6 Oct). *Endangered Species.* T **195** *and similar horiz designs. Multicoloured.* W w **16** (*sideways*). P 14½.

795	17p. Type **195**	90	65
796	19p. Southern Sealion	90	75
797	40p. Felton's Flower	1·50	1·50
798	73p. Trout	2·50	3·00
795/8	Set of 4	5·25	5·50

(Des N. Shewring. Litho Questa)

1998 (26 Feb). *Centenary of Falkland Islands Fire Service.* T **196** *and similar vert designs. Multicoloured.* W w **16**. P 14½×14.

799	9p. Type **196**	55	45
800	17p. Merryweather's Hatfield trailer pump	80	60
801	40p. Coventry Climax Godiva trailer pump	1·50	1·50
802	65p. Carmichael Bedford "Type B" water tender	2·25	2·50
799/802	Set of 4	4·50	4·50

196*a* Diana, Princess of Wales, 1990

(Des D. Miller. Litho Questa)

1998 (31 Mar). *Diana, Princess of Wales Commemoration. Sheet,* 145×70 *mm, containing* T **196***a and similar vert designs. Multicoloured.* W w **14** (*sideways*). P 14½×14.
MS803   30p. Type **196***a*; 30p. Wearing red dress, 1988; 30p. Resting head on hand, 1991; 30p. Wearing landmine protection clothing, Angola (*sold at* £1.20 + 20p. *charity premium*) ..   3·25   3·25

197 Tawny-throated Dotterel   **198** *Penelope* (auxiliary ketch)

(Des A. Robinson. Litho Questa)

1998 (14 July). *Rare Visiting Birds.* T **197** *and similar horiz designs. Multicoloured.* W w **14** (*sideways*). P 14.

(*a*) *Designs* 39½×23½ *mm*

804	1p. Type **197**	10	10
805	2p. Hudsonian Godwit	10	10
806	5p. Eared Dove	10	10
807	9p. Great Grebe	20	25
808	10p. Chilian Lapwing ("Southern Lapwing")	20	25
809	16p. Buff-necked Ibis	30	35
810	30p. Ashy-headed Goose	60	65
811	65p. Red-legged Cormorant ("Red-legged Shag")	1·25	1·40
812	88p. Argentine Shoveler ("Red Shoveler")	1·75	1·90
813	£1 Red-fronted Coot	2·00	2·10
814	£3 Chilian Flamingo	6·00	6·25
815	£5 Fork-tailed Flycatcher	10·00	10·50

(*b*) *Booklet stamps. Designs* 35×22 *mm*
816	9p. Roseate Spoonbill	20	25
	a. Booklet pane. Nos. 816×2, 817×8 and 2 stamp-size labels	3·00	

817	17p. Austral Conure ("Austral Parakeet")	35	40
818	35p. American Kestrel	70	75
	a. Booklet pane. No. 818×6	4·00	
804/18	Set of 15	23·00	24·00

(Des R. Yssel. Litho Questa)

1998 (30 Sept). *Local Vessels.* T **198** *and similar multicoloured designs.* W w **14** (*sideways*). P 14.

819	17p. Type **198**	65	55
820	35p. *Ilen* (auxiliary ketch)	1·25	1·25
821	40p. *Weddell* (schooner)	1·40	1·40
822	65p. *Lively* (tug) (31×22 *mm*)	1·90	2·00
819/22	Set of 4	4·75	4·75

199 First Medivac Air Ambulance Service, 1948   **200** Marine at Port Egmont, Saunders Island, 1766

(Des N. Shewring. Litho Questa)

1998 (30 Oct). 50*th Anniv of Falkland Islands Government Air Service.* T **199** *and similar horiz design. Multicoloured.* W w **14** (*sideways*). P 14.
823	17p. Type **199**	60	50
824	£1 F.I.G.A.S. Beaver and Islander aircraft over map	2·50	2·50

(Des V. Ambrus. Litho Walsall)

1998 (8 Dec). *Royal Marine Uniforms.* T **200** *and similar vert designs. Multicoloured.* W w **14**. P 14½×14.

825	17p. Type **200**	55	55
826	30p. Officer at Port Louis, East Falklands, 1833	85	85
827	35p. Corporal and H.M.S. *Kent* (cruiser), 1914	90	90
828	65p. Bugler at Government House, 1976	1·75	2·00
825/8	Set of 4	3·50	3·75

201 Altar, St. Mary's Church

(Des J. Peck. Litho Walsall)

1999 (12 Feb). *Centenary of St. Mary's Roman Catholic Church, Stanley.* T **201** *and similar horiz designs. Multicoloured.* W w **16** (*sideways*). P 14.
829	17p. Type **201**	45	45
830	40p. St. Mary's Church	1·00	1·10
831	75p. Laying of foundation stone, 1899	1·75	2·10
829/31	Set of 3	2·75	3·25

NEW INFORMATION

The editor is always interested to correspond with people who have new information that will improve or correct the Catalogue.

26 — Falkland Islands　　　　　　　　　　　　　　　　　　　　1999

202 H.M.S. *Beagle* (Darwin)　　203 Prince of Wales (from photo by Clive Arrowsmith)

(Des R. Watton. Litho Walsall)

1999 (5 Mar). "*Australia '99*" *World Stamp Exhibition, Melbourne. Maritime History.* T **202** *and similar horiz designs. Multicoloured.* W w **16** (*sideways*). P 14.

832	25p. Type **202**	..	70	70
833	35p. H.M.A.S. *Australia* (battle cruiser)	..	90	90
834	40p. *Canberra* (liner)	..	1·00	1·00
835	50p. *Great Britain* (steam/sail)	..	1·25	1·50
	a. Horiz pair. Nos. 835/6		2·50	3·00
836	50p. All-England Cricket Team, 1861–62		1·25	1·50
832/6		Set of 5	4·50	5·00

Nos. 835/6 were printed together, *se-tenant*, in horizontal pairs throughout the sheet.

(Des and litho Walsall)

1999 (13 Mar). *Royal Visit.* W w **16**. P 14×13½.
837　**203**　£2 multicoloured　..　..　..　4·50　4·75

203a Prince Edward and Miss Sophie Rhys-Jones

(Des D. Miller. Litho Walsall)

1999 (15 June). *Royal Wedding.* T **203a** *and similar vert designs. Multicoloured.* W w **16**. P 14.

838	80p. Type **203a**	..	1·75	1·90
839	£1.20, Engagement photograph	..	2·75	3·00

204 *Jeanne d'Arc* (French cruiser)

(Des J. Batchelor. Litho Questa)

1999 (21 June). "*PhilexFrance '99*" *International Stamp Exhibition, Paris. First Flight over Falkland Islands, 1931.* T **204** *and similar horiz designs. Multicoloured.* W w **14** (*sideways*). P 14.

840	35p. Type **204**	..	90	90
841	40p. CAMS 37 (flying boat) taking off	..	90	90
MS842	115×63 mm. £1 CAMS 37 over Port Stanley (47×31 *mm*). P 13½×14	..	2·25	2·25

204a Queen Elizabeth visiting Ship, Port of London, 1939

(Des D. Miller. Litho Cartor)

1999 (18 Aug). "*Queen Elizabeth the Queen Mother's Century*". T **204a** *and similar horiz designs. Multicoloured.* W w **16** (*sideways*). P 13½.

843	9p. Type **204a**	..	30	30
844	20p. With Queen Elizabeth II, 1996	..	55	55
845	30p. With Prince Charles and his sons, 1995		75	75
846	67p. Presenting colours to Queen's Royal Hussars	..	1·75	1·75
843/6		Set of 4	3·00	3·00
MS847	145×70 mm. £1.40, Duchess of York, 1936, and Shackleton, Scott and Wilson in the Antarctic, 1902		3·50	3·75

205 Chiloe Wigeon　　　206 Hulk of *Vicar of Bray*, 1999

(Des I. Strange. Litho Walsall)

1999 (9 Sept). *Waterfowl.* T **205** *and similar horiz designs. Multicoloured.* W w **16** (*sideways*). P 14×14½.

848	9p. Type **205**	..	30	30
849	17p. Crested Duck	..	55	55
850	30p. Georgian Teal ("Brown Pintail")	..	75	75
851	35p. Versicolor Teal ("Silver Teal")	..	80	80
852	40p. Chilean Teal ("Yellow-billed Teal")	..	95	95
853	65p. Falkland Islands Flightless Steamer Duck	..	1·60	1·60
848/53		Set of 6	4·50	4·50

(Litho Questa)

1999 (3 Nov). *150th Anniv of California Goldrush.* T **206** *and similar horiz designs.* W w **14** (*sideways*). *Multicoloured.* P 14.

854	9p. Type **206**	..	40	40
855	35p. Panning for gold, 1849	..	90	90
856	40p. Gold rocking cradle, 1849	..	95	95
857	80p. *Vicar of Bray* (barque) at sea, 1849	..	1·90	1·90
854/7		Set of 4	3·75	3·75
MS858	105×63 mm. £1 *Vicar of Bray* in San Francisco (47×31 *mm*). P 13½	..	2·00	2·10

1999   Falkland Islands — 27

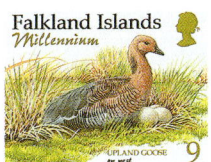  

207 Magellan Goose on Nest 208 Princess Alexandra and Meadow

208c Prince William wearing Fireman's Helmet, 1988

(Des A. Robinson. Litho Questa)

1999 (6 Dec). *New Millennium.* T **207** *and similar horiz designs. Multicoloured.* W w **14** (*sideways*). P 14½.

859	9p. Type **207**			20	25
860	9p. Kelp Gull at sunrise			20	25
861	9p. Christ Church Cathedral, Stanley			20	25
862	30p. Night Heron at sunset			60	65
863	30p. Family and Christmas tree			60	65
864	30p. King Penguins			60	65
859/64			Set of 6	2·40	2·75

(Des D. Miller. Litho Cartor)

2000 (1 Feb). *Visit of Princess Alexandra.* T **208** *and similar horiz design. Multicoloured.* W w **14** (*sideways*). P 13½.

865	9p. Type **208**			20	25
866	£1 Princess Alexandra and plantation of saplings			2·00	2·10

208a *Endurance* off Caird Coast   208b Queen Elizabeth I

(Des M. Skidmore. Litho Questa)

2000 (10 Feb). *Shackleton's Trans-Antarctic Expedition, 1914–17, Commemoration.* T **208a** *and similar horiz designs.* W w **14** (*sideways*). P 14.

867	17p. multicoloured			35	40
868	45p. grey-blue and black			90	95
869	75p. multicoloured			1·50	1·75
867/9			Set of 3	2·75	3·00

Designs—45p. *Endurance* beset in the Weddell Sea pack-ice; 75p. Sir Ernest Shackleton and *Yelcho* (Chilean rescue tug).

(Des Crown Agents. Litho Walsall)

2000 (29 Feb). *"The Stamp Show* 2000" *International Stamp Exhibition, London. Kings and Queens of England.* T **208b** *and similar vert designs. Multicoloured.* W w **14**. P 14.

870	40p. Type **208b**			80	85
	a. Sheetlet. Nos. 870/5			4·75	
871	40p. King James II			80	85
872	40p. King George I			80	85
873	40p. King William IV			80	85
874	40p. King Edward VIII			80	85
875	40p. Queen Elizabeth II			80	85
870/5			Set of 6	4·75	5·00

Nos. 870/5 were printed together *se-tenant*, in sheetlets of 6 with an enlarged illustrated right-hand margin.

(Des A. Robinson. Litho Questa)

2000 (21 June). *18th Birthday of Prince William.* T **208c** *and similar multicoloured designs.* W w **14** (*sideways on* 10p. *and* 20p.). P 14×14½ (*vert*) *or* 14½×14 (*horiz*).

876	10p. Type **208c**			20	25
877	20p. At Eton, 1995			40	45
878	37p. Prince William in Cardiff, 2000 (*horiz*)			75	80
879	43p. Prince William in 1998 (*horiz*)			85	90
876/9			Set of 4	2·10	2·40
MS880	175×95 mm. 50p. With Golden Retriever, 1997 (*horiz*) and Nos. 876/9. Wmk sideways. P 14½			3·00	3·25

2000 (4 Aug). *Queen Elizabeth the Queen Mother's 100th Birthday. No.* **MS**847 *optd* "100 birthday" *die-stamped in gold foil.*

MS881 145×70 mm. £1.40, Duchess of York, 1936, and Shackleton, Scott and Wilson in the Antarctic, 1902 .. 2·75 3·00

No. **MS**881 also has "100TH BIRTHDAY OF HM QUEEN ELIZABETH THE QUEEN MOTHER" die-stamped in gold foil on the bottom sheet margin.

STAMP BOOKLETS

1977 (1 Nov). *Silver Jubilee. Multicoloured cover,* 117×79 *mm, showing Norroy and Ulster King of Arms. Stapled.*
SB1 £2 booklet containing 6p., 11p. and 33p., each in pane of 4 (Nos. 326a, 327a, 327ba) .. 10·00

1978 (27 Nov). *Mail Ships. Black and blue-green cover,* 99×57 *mm, showing* Hebe *on front and* Darwin *on back. Stapled.*
SB2 £1 booklet containing 1p., 3p., 5p., 6p., 10p. (Nos. 331A, 333A, 335A/6A, 340A) each in block of 4 24·00

1979 (4 June). *Mail Ships. Black and bright new blue cover,* 99×57 *mm, showing* Nautilus *on front and* A.E.S. *on back. Stapled.*
SB3 £1 booklet. Contents as No. SB2 .. 11·00

1980 (14 July). *Mail Ships. Black and red cover,* 100×59 *mm, showing* Amelia *on front and* Merak-N *on back. Stapled.*
SB4 £1 booklet. Contents as No. SB2 .. 5·50

1982 (23 Feb). *Mail Ships. Black and grey cover,* 99×58 *mm, showing* Fairy *on front and* Fitzroy *on back. Stapled.*
SB5 £1 booklet. Contents as No. SB2 .. 4·75

1985 (18 Feb). *Black and azure cover,* 95×64 *mm, with example of stamp No.* 471A *affixed. Stapled.*
SB6 £2.24, booklet containing eight 2p. and four each 7p., 20p., 25p. (Nos. 470A, 475A, 479A, 480A) in blocks of 4 .. 21·00

1988 (2 Feb). *Black and greenish grey cover,* 95×64 *mm, with example of stamp No.* 470A *affixed. Stapled.*
SB7 £2.52, booklet containing eight 4p. and four each 10p., 20p., 25p. (Nos. 472A, 478A/80A) in blocks of 4 .. 15·00

28 — Falkland Islands

1988 (26 Sept). *Black and pale green cover, 95×64 mm, with example of stamp No. 471A affixed. Stapled.*
SB8   £2.52, booklet containing 1p., 4p., 6p., 8p., 9p., 10p., 25p. (Nos. 469A, 472A, 474A, 476A/8A, 480A), each in block of 4 .. .. .. 7·00

1990 (29 Oct). *Cape Horn Sailing Ships. Black and greenish yellow showing No. 575 (No. SB9) or pale blue showing No. 578 (No. SB10) covers, each 104×55 mm. Panes attached by selvedge.*
SB9   60p. booklet containing 3p., 9p. (Nos. 569, 575), each in block of 5 .. .. .. 7·50
SB10   £1.55, booklet containing 6p., 25p. (Nos. 572, 578), each in block of 5 .. .. .. 9·00

1998 (14 July). *Rare Visiting Birds. Multicoloured covers, 86×52 mm, showing Roseate Spoonbill (No. SB11) or American Kestrel (No. SB12). Panes attached by selvedge.*
SB11   £1.54, booklet containing pane of two 9p., eight 17p. and 2 stamp-size labels (No. 816a) .. 3·00
SB12   £2.10, booklet containing pane of six 35p. (No. 818a) .. .. 4·25

POSTAGE DUE STAMPS

D 1 King Penguin

(Des O. Bell. Litho Questa)

1991 (7 Jan). W w **14** (*sideways*). P 15×14.

D1	D 1	1p.	brown-lake and cerise	10	10
D2		2p.	red-orange and pale orange	10	10
D3		3p.	brown-ochre and chrome-yellow	10	10
D4		4p.	deep blue-green & light blue-green	10	10
D5		5p.	greenish blue & light greenish blue	10	15
D6		10p.	deep violet-blue and cobalt	20	25
D7		20p.	deep reddish violet and lilac	40	45
D8		50p.	yellowish green and apple-green	1·00	1·10
D1/8			Set of 8	1·90	2·10

Falkland Islands Dependencies — 29

FALKLAND ISLANDS DEPENDENCIES

PRICES FOR STAMPS ON COVER TO 1945
Nos. A1/D8   *from* × 20

A. GRAHAM LAND

For use at Port Lockroy (established 16 February 1944) and Hope Bay (established 12 February 1945) bases.
Falkland Islands definitive stamps with face values of 1s. 3d. and above were valid for use from Graham Land in conjunction with Nos. A1/8 and subsequently Nos. G1/16.

Stamps of FALKLAND ISLANDS *cancelled at Port Lockroy or Hope Bay with Graham Land circular datestamps between* 16 February 1944 *and* 31 January 1954.

1938–50. *King George VI (Nos. 159/63).*
Z1	1s. 3d. black and carmine-red	75·00
Z2	2s. 6d. slate	30·00
Z3	5s. indigo and yellow-brown	£130
Z4	10s. black and orange	40·00
Z5	£1 black and violet	60·00

1952. *King George VI (Nos. 181/5)*
Z 6	1s. 3d. orange	
Z 7	2s. 6d. olive-green	
Z 8	5s. purple	
Z 9	10s. grey	
Z10	£1 black	

GRAHAM LAND

DEPENDENCY OF
(A 1)

1944 (12 Feb)–**45.** *Falkland Islands Nos.* 146, 148, 150, 153/5, 157 *and* 158a *optd with Type* A 1, *in red, by B.W.*

A1	½d. black and green	30	1·75
	a. Blue-black and green	£600	£375
A2	1d. black and violet	30	1·00
A3	2d. black and carmine-red	40	1·00
A4	3d. black and blue	30	1·00
A5	4d. black and purple	3·00	1·75
A6	6d. black and brown	14·00	2·25
	a. Blue-black and brown (24.9.45)	20·00	
A7	9d. black and grey-blue	1·00	1·25
A8	1s. deep blue	1·00	1·25
A1/8		Set of 8 18·00	10·00
A1/8 Perf "Specimen"		Set of 8 £325	

B. SOUTH GEORGIA

The stamps of Falkland Islands were used at the Grytviken whaling station on South Georgia from 3 December 1909.
Mr. J. Innes Wilson, the Stipendary Magistrate whose duties included those of postmaster, was issued with a stock of stamps, values ½d. to 5s., together with an example of the current "FALKLAND ISLANDS" circular datestamp. This was used to cancel the stamps, but, as it gave no indication that mail had originated at South Georgia, a straight-line handstamp inscribed "SOUTH GEORGIA", or subsequently "South Georgia", was also supplied. It was intended that this should be struck directly on to each letter or card below the stamp, but it can sometimes be found struck across the stamp instead.
The use of the "South Georgia" handstamp continued after the introduction of the "SOUTH GEORGIA" circular datestamp in June 1910 apparently for philatelic purposes, but no example has been reported used after June 1912.

SOUTH GEORGIA.
Z 1

South Georgia.
Z 2

		On piece	On cover /card
ZU1	Example of Type Z 1 used in conjunction with "FALKLAND ISLANDS" postmark (22 Dec 1909 to 30 March 1910) *Price from*	£1000	£3750
ZU2	Example of Type Z 2 used in conjunction with "FALKLAND ISLANDS" postmark (May 1910) .. .. *Price from*	£750	£3000
ZU3	Example of Type Z 2 used in conjunction with "SOUTH GEORGIA" postmark (June 1910 to June 1912) .. *Price from*	£250	£900

Stamps of FALKLAND ISLANDS *cancelled at Grytviken with South Georgia circular datestamps between* June 1910 *and* 31 January 1954.

1891–1902. *Queen Victoria (Nos. 32, 36 and 38).*
Z11	4d. olive-black	£140
Z12	9d. salmon	£140
Z13	1s. yellow-brown	£150

1904–12. *King Edward VII (Nos. 43/50).*
Z14	½d. green	11·00
Z15	1d. vermilion	11·00
	d. Dull coppery red (on thick paper)	35·00
Z16	2d. purple	50·00
	b. Reddish purple	£275
Z17	2½d. ultramarine	20·00
	b. Deep blue	£180
Z18	6d. orange	£100
Z19	1s. brown	£100
Z20	3s. green	£200
Z21	5s. red	£250

SOUTH GEORGIA PROVISIONAL HANDSTAMPS. During October 1911 the arrival of the German South Polar Expedition at Grytviken, South Georgia, resulted in the local supply of stamps becoming exhausted. The Acting Magistrate, Mr. E. B. Binnie, who was also responsible for the postal facilities, produced a handstamp reading "Paid at (or At) SOUTH GEORGIA" which, together with a manuscript indication of the postage paid and his signature, was used on mail from 18 October 1911 to January 1912. Further examples, signed by John Innes Wilson, are known from February 1912, but these may be philatelic.

PH1 "Paid 1 at SOUTH GEORGIA EBB" *Price on cover* £4250
PH1*a* "Paid 1 At SOUTH GEORGIA EBB" (16 Dec)
Price on cover £4500
PH2 "Paid 2½ at SOUTH GEORGIA EBB" *Price on cover* £4750
PH2*a* "Paid 2½ At SOUTH GEORGIA EBB" (16 Dec)
Price on cover £5250

1912–23. *King George V. Wmk Mult Crown CA (Nos. 60/9).*
Z22	½d. green	15·00
	a. Perf 14 (line). *Deep yellow-green*	35·00
	d. Dull yellowish green (on thick greyish paper)	30·00
Z23	1d. orange-red	10·00
	a. Perf 14 (line). *Orange-vermilion*	10·00
	d. Orange-vermilion	10·00
Z24	2d. maroon	40·00
Z25	2½d. deep bright blue	25·00
	c. Deep blue	25·00
Z26	6d. yellow-orange	50·00
	b. Brown-orange	45·00
	ba. Bisected (diag) (3d.) (on cover) (3.23)	£11000
Z27	1s. bistre-brown	£100
	b. Brown (on thick greyish paper)	£150
Z28	3s. slate-green	£150
Z29	5s. deep rose-red	£180
	a. Reddish maroon	£275
	b. Maroon	£225
Z30	10s. red/*green*	£300
Z31	£1 black/*red*	£450

1918–20. "WAR STAMP" *ovpts (Nos. 70/2).*
Z32	½d. deep olive	15·00
Z33	1d. vermilion	15·00
Z34	1s. light bistre-brown	80·00

30 — Falkland Islands Dependencies

1921–28. *King George V. Wmk Mult Script CA (Nos. 73/80).*
Z35	½d. yellowish green	5·00
Z36	1d. dull vermilion	4·00
Z37	2d. deep brown-purple	25·00
Z38	2½d. deep blue	22·00
	a. Bisected (diag) (1d.) (on cover) (3.21)	£7000
	b. Prussian blue	£450
Z39	2½d. deep purple/*pale yellow*	45·00
Z40	6d. yellow-orange	50·00
Z41	1s. deep ochre	60·00
Z42	3s. slate-green	£160

1928 PROVISIONAL. For listing of the 2½d. on 2d. surcharge issued at Grytviken on 7 February 1928 see No. 115 of Falkland Islands.

1929–36. *King George V. Whale and Penguins design (Nos. 116/26).*
Z43	½d. green	5·00
Z44	1d. scarlet	4·00
Z45	2d. grey	10·00
Z46	2½d. blue	4·00
Z47	4d. orange	20·00
Z48	6d. purple	30·00
Z49	1s. black/*emerald*	35·00
Z50	2s. 6d. carmine/*blue*	75·00
Z51	5s. green/*yellow*	£110
Z52	10s. carmine/*emerald*	£200
Z53	£1 black/*red*	£500

Examples of most values are known with forged postmarks dated "Au 30" in 1928, 1930 and 1931.

1933. *Centenary of British Administration (Nos. 127/38).*
Z54	½d. black and green	7·00
Z55	1d. black and scarlet	4·00
Z56	1½d. black and blue	16·00
Z57	2d. black and brown	26·00
Z58	3d. black and violet	17·00
Z59	4d. black and orange	19·00
Z60	6d. black and slate	70·00
Z61	1s. black and olive-green	65·00
Z62	2s. 6d. black and violet	£200
Z63	5s. black and yellow	£750
	a. Black and yellow-orange	£1400
Z64	10s. black and chestnut	£850
Z65	£1 black and carmine	£2250

1935. *Silver Jubilee (Nos. 139/42).*
Z66	1d. deep blue and scarlet	3·00
Z67	2½d. brown and deep blue	4·00
Z68	4d. green and indigo	5·00
Z69	1s. slate and purple	5·00

1937. *Coronation (Nos. 143/5).*
Z70	½d. green	2·00
Z71	1d. carmine	2·00
Z72	2½d. blue	2·00

1938–50. *King George VI (Nos. 146/63).*
Z73	½d. black and green	3·00
Z74	1d. black and carmine	5·00
	a. Black and scarlet	2·00
Z75	1d. black and violet	4·50
Z76	2d. black and deep violet	6·00
Z77	2d. black and carmine-red	7·00
Z78	2½d. black and bright blue (No. 151)	2·00
Z79	3d. black and blue	6·00
Z80	4d. black and purple	6·00
Z81	6d. black and brown	8·00
Z82	9d. black and grey-blue	10·00
Z83	1s. pale blue	30·00
	a. Deep blue	30·00
Z84	1s. 3d. black and carmine-red	30·00
Z85	2s. 6d. slate	20·00
Z86	5s. bright blue and pale brown	£100
	a. Indigo and yellow-brown	£130
	b. Blue and buff-brown	£200
Z87	10s. black and orange	40·00
Z88	£1 black and violet	60·00

Falkland Islands definitive stamps with values of 1s. 3d. above continued to be valid from South Georgia after the introduction of Nos. B1/8 and subsequently Nos. G1/16.

1952. *King George VI (Nos. 181/5).*
Z89	1s. 3d. orange	25·00
Z90	2s. 6d. olive-green	
Z91	5s. purple	
Z92	10s. grey	
Z93	£1 black	

1944 (24 Feb)–45. *Falkland Islands Nos. 146, 148, 150, 153/5, 157 and 158a optd "SOUTH GEORGIA/DEPENDENCY OF", in red, as Type A 1 of Graham Land.*
B1	½d. black and green	30	1·75
	a. Wmk sideways	£2750	
B2	1d. black and violet	30	1·00
B3	2d. black and carmine-red	40	1·00
B4	3d. black and blue	30	1·00
B5	4d. black and purple	3·00	1·75
B6	6d. black and brown	14·00	2·25
	a. Blue-black and brown (24.9.45)	20·00	
B7	9d. black and grey-blue	1·00	1·25
B8	1s. deep blue	1·00	1·00
B1/8		Set of 8 18·00	10·00
B1/8 Perf "Specimen"		Set of 8 £325	

For later issues, see after No. G44.

C. SOUTH ORKNEYS

Used from the *Fitzroy* in February 1944 and at Laurie Island (established January 1946).

Falkland Islands definitive stamps with face values of 1s. 3d. and above were valid for use from the South Orkneys in conjunction with Nos. C1/8 and subsequently Nos. G1/16.

Stamps of FALKLAND ISLANDS *cancelled on the* Fitzroy, *at Laurie Island or at Signy Island with South Orkneys circular datestamps between* 21 February 1944 *and* 31 January 1954.

1938–50. *King George VI (Nos. 160/3).*
Z95	2s. 6d. slate	30·00
Z96	5s. indigo and yellow-brown	£130
Z97	10s. black and orange	40·00
Z98	£1 black and violet	60·00

1952. *King George VI (Nos. 181/5).*
Z 99	1s. 3d. orange	
Z100	2s. 6d. olive-green	
Z101	5s. purple	
Z102	10s. grey	
Z103	£1 black	

1944 (21 Feb)–45. *Falkland Islands Nos. 146, 148, 150, 153/5, 157 and 158a optd* "SOUTH ORKNEYS/DEPENDENCY OF", *in red as Type A 1 of Graham Land.*
C1	½d. black and green	30	1·75
C2	1d. black and violet	30	1·00
	w. Wmk inverted	£3750	
C3	2d. black and carmine-red	40	1·00
C4	3d. black and blue	30	1·00
C5	4d. black and purple	3·00	1·75
C6	6d. black and brown	14·00	2·25
	a. Blue-black and brown (24.9.45)	20·00	
C7	9d. black and grey-blue	1·00	1·25
C8	1s. deep blue	1·00	1·25
C1/8		Set of 8 18·00	10·00
C1/8 Perf "Specimen"		Set of 8 £325	

D. SOUTH SHETLANDS

Postal facilities were first provided at the Port Foster whaling station on Deception Island for the 1912–13 whaling season and were available each year between November and the following April until March 1931.

No postmark was provided for the 1912–13 season and the local postmaster was instructed to cancel stamps on cover with a straight-line "PORT FOSTER" handstamp. Most letters so cancelled subsequently received a "FALKLAND ISLANDS" circular postmark dated between 19 and 28 March 1913. It is known that only low value stamps were available at Port Foster. Higher values, often with other "FALKLAND ISLANDS" postmark dates, were, it is believed, subsequently "made to order".

Falkland Islands Dependencies — 31

Stamps of FALKLAND ISLANDS *cancelled at Port Foster, Deception Island with part of* "PORT FOSTER" *straight-line handstamp.*

1904–12. *King Edward VII (Nos. 43/4).*
Z104   ½d. deep yellow-green £1200
Z105   1d. orange-vermilion £1200

1912. *King George V. Wmk Mult Crown CA (No. 60).*
Z106   ½d. yellow-green £1200

Stamps of FALKLAND ISLANDS *cancelled at Port Foster with part of oval* "DECEPTION ISLAND SOUTH SHETLANDS" *postmark in black or violet between* 1914 *and* 1927.

1904–12. *King Edward VII (No. 43B).*
Z108   ½d. deep yellow-green £200

1912–20. *King George V. Wmk Mult Crown CA (Nos. 60/9).*
Z110   ½d. yellow-green .. .. .. 75·00
Z111   1d. orange-red .. .. .. 75·00
Z112   2d. maroon £100
Z113   2½d. deep bright blue £100
Z114   6d. yellow-orange £120
Z115   1s. light bistre-brown £140
Z116   3s. slate-green £300
Z117   5s. deep rose-red £350
Z118   10s. red/*green* £450
Z119   £1 black/*red* £600

1918–20. "WAR STAMP" *ovpts (Nos. 70/2).*
Z120   ½d. deep olive £100
Z121   1d. vermilion £100
Z122   1s. light bistre-brown £200

1921–28. *King George V. Wmk Mult Script CA (Nos. 73/80).*
Z123   ½d. yellowish green £100
Z126   2½d. deep blue £130
Z129   1s. deep ochre £150

Stamps of FALKLAND ISLANDS *cancelled at Port Foster with* "SOUTH SHETLANDS" *circular datestamp between* 1923 *and* March 1931

1912–20. *King George V. Wmk Mult Crown CA (Nos. 60/9).*
Z130   1d. orange-vermilion .. .. .. 50·00
Z131   2d. deep reddish purple .. .. .. 60·00
Z132   2½d. deep bright blue ..
Z133   6d. brown-orange .. .. .. 80·00
Z134   1s. bistre-brown ..
Z135   3s. slate-green £160
Z136   5s. maroon £180
Z137   10s. red/*green* £325
Z138   £1 black/*red* £550
Examples of all values are known with forged postmarks dated "20 MR 27".

1918–20. "WAR STAMP" *ovpts (Nos. 70/2).*
Z139   1d. vermilion
Z140   1s. light bistre brown

1921–28. *King George V. Wmk Mult Script CA (Nos. 73/80).*
Z141   ½d. yellowish green .. .. .. 35·00
Z142   1d. dull vermilion .. .. .. 35·00
Z143   2d. deep brown-purple .. .. .. 50·00
Z144   2½d. deep blue .. .. .. 40·00
Z145   2½d. deep purple/*pale yellow* .. .. 75·00
Z146   6d. yellow-orange .. .. .. 60·00
Z147   1s. deep ochre .. .. .. 60·00
Z148   3s. slate-green £170

1929. *King George V. Whale and Penguins design (Nos. 116/26).*
Z149   ½d. green .. .. .. 50·00
Z150   1d. scarlet .. .. .. 50·00
Z151   2d. grey .. .. .. 70·00
Z152   2½d. blue .. .. .. 60·00
Z153   6d. purple .. .. .. 80·00
Z154   1s. black/*emerald* .. .. .. 80·00
Z155   2s. 6d. carmine/*blue* £120
Z156   5s. green/*yellow* £130
Z157   10s. carmine/*emerald* £275
Z158   £1 black/*red* £500

The whaling station at Port Foster was abandoned at the end of the 1930–31 season.
It was reoccupied as a Falkland Islands Dependencies Survey base on 3 February 1944.
Falkland Islands definitive stamps with face values of 1s. 3d. and above were valid for use from the South Shetlands in conjunction with Nos. D1/8 and subsequently Nos. G1/16.

Stamps of FALKLAND ISLANDS *cancelled at Port Foster or Admiralty Bay with South Shetlands circular datestamps between* 5 February 1944 *and* 31 January 1954

1938–50. *King George VI (Nos. 160/3).*
Z159   2s. 6d. slate .. .. .. 30·00
Z160   5s. indigo and yellow-brown £130
Z161   10s. black and orange .. .. .. 40·00
Z162   £1 black and violet .. .. .. 60·00

1952. *King George VI (Nos. 181/5).*
Z163   1s. 3d. orange ..
Z164   2s. 6d. olive-green ..
Z165   5s. purple ..
Z166   10s. grey ..
Z167   £1 black

1944 (5 Feb)–45. *Falkland Islands Nos. 146, 148, 150, 153/5, 157 and 158a optd* "SOUTH SHETLANDS/DEPENDENCY OF", *in red, as Type A 1 of Graham Land.*
D1   ½d. black and green 30   1·75
D2   1d. black and violet 30   1·00
D3   2d. black and carmine-red 40   1·00
D4   3d. black and blue 30   1·00
D5   4d. black and purple .. .. 3·00   1·75
D6   6d. black and brown .. .. 14·00   2·25
  a. Blue-black and brown (24.9.45) .. 20·00
D7   9d. black and grey-blue .. .. 1·00   1·25
D8   1s. deep blue .. .. 1·00   1·25
D1/8   .. .. .. Set of 8   18·00   10·00
D1/8 Perf "Specimen" .. .. Set of 8   £325

From 12 July 1946 to 16 July 1963, Graham Land, South Georgia, South Orkneys and South Shetlands used FALKLAND ISLANDS DEPENDENCIES stamps.

E. FALKLAND ISLANDS DEPENDENCIES

For use at the following bases:
Adelaide Island (Graham Land) (*opened* 1961)
Admiralty Bay (South Shetlands) (*opened* January 1948, *closed* January 1961)
Anvers Island (Graham Land) (*opened* February 1955, *closed* 10 January 1958)
Argentine Islands (Graham Land) (*opened* 1947)
Danco Coast ("Base O") (Graham Land) (*opened* 30 March 1956, *closed* 1958)
Deception Island (South Shetlands)
Grytviken (South Georgia)
Halley Bay (Coats Land) (*opened* 1956)
Hope Bay (Graham Land) (*closed* 4 February 1949, *opened* February 1952)
Laurie Island (South Orkneys) (*closed* 1947)
Loubet Coast ("Base W") (Graham Land) (*opened* 1955, *closed* 1959)
Marguerite Bay (Graham Land) (*opened* March 1955, *closed* 1960)
Port Lockroy (Graham Land) (*closed* 16 January 1962)
Prospect Point ("Base J") (Graham Land) (*opened* 1956, *closed* 1958)
Shackleton (Coats Land) (*opened* 1956, *closed* 1957)
Signy Island (South Orkneys) (*opened* 1946)
Stonington Island (Graham Land) (*opened* 1946, *closed* 1950, *opened* 1958, *closed* 1959, *opened* 1960)

32 — Falkland Islands Dependencies 1946

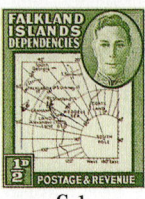
G 1

On Nos. G9 to G16 the map is redrawn; the "o°" meridian does not pass through the "S" of "COATS", the "n" of "Alexander" is not joined to the "L" of "Land" below, and the loops of letters "s" and "t" are generally more open.

(Map litho, frame recess D.L.R.)

1946 (12 July*)—49. *Wmk Mult Script CA (sideways). P 12.*

(a) Map thick and coarse

G 1	G 1	½d. black and green	..	1·00	2·25
		a. Extra island ..	..	65·00	
		b. Missing "I"	..	65·00	
		c. "SOUTH POKE"	..	65·00	
G 2		1d. black and violet	..	1·25	1·75
		a. Extra island ..	..	65·00	
		b. Missing "I"	..	65·00	
G 3		2d. black and carmine	..	1·25	2·50
		a. Extra island ..	..	70·00	
		b. Missing "I"	..	70·00	
G 4		3d. black and blue	..	1·25	4·00
		a. Extra island ..	..	80·00	
		b. Missing "I"	..	80·00	
G 5		4d. black and claret	..	2·25	4·75
		c. "SOUTH POKE"	..	95·00	
G 6		6d. black and orange	..	3·25	4·75
		a. Extra island ..	..	£110	
		b. Missing "I"	..	£110	
		c. "SOUTH POKE"	..	£110	
		d. *Black and ochre*	..	48·00	90·00
		da. Extra island ..	..	£275	
		db. Missing "I"	..	£275	
		dc. "SOUTH POKE"	..	£275	
G 7		9d. black and brown	..	2·00	3·75
		c. "SOUTH POKE"	..	95·00	
G 8		1s. black and purple	..	2·00	4·25
		c. "SOUTH POKE"	..	95·00	
G1/8		.. .. ..	*Set of* 8	13·00	25·00
G1/8 Perf "Specimen"			*Set of* 8	£450	

Extra island (Plate 1 R. 3/9)

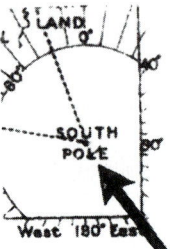
"SOUTH POKE" flaw (Plate 2 R. 6/8)

(b) Map thin and clear (16.2.48)

G 9	G 1	½d. black and green	..	2·25	11·00
		a. Recess frame printed double, one albino and inverted ..	..	£900	
G10		1d. black and violet	..	1·50	14·00
G11		2d. black and carmine	..	3·75	19·00
G11a		2½d. black and deep blue (6.3.49)	..	7·50	7·00
G12		3d. black and blue ..	..	2·75	4·50
G13		4d. black and claret	..	16·00	20·00
G14		6d. black and orange	..	23·00	11·00
G15		9d. black and brown	..	23·00	10·00
G16		1s. black and purple	..	23·00	10·00
G9/16		.. ..	*Set of* 9	90·00	95·00

*This is the date of issue for South Georgia. Nos. G1/8 were released in London on 11 February.

In Nos. G1/8 a variety with a gap in the 80th parallel occurs six times in each sheet of all values in positions R. 1/4, 1/9, 3/4, 3/9, 5/4 and 5/9 (*Price for set of 8 £40 mint, in pairs with normal*).

A constant variety, dot on "T" of "SOUTH", occurs on R. 5/2, 5/4, 5/6, 5/8 and 5/10 of all values of the "thin map" set with the exception of the 2½d.

Missing "I" in "S. Shetland Is." (Plate 1 R. 1/2)

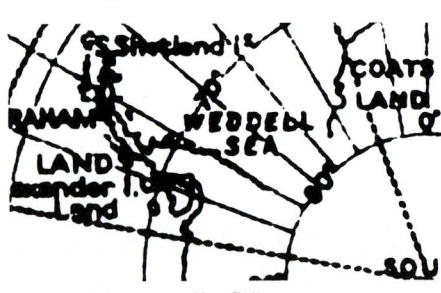
Nos. G1/8

1946 (4 Oct*). *Victory. As Nos. 164/5 of Falkland Islands.*

G17		1d. deep violet	..	50	15
G18		3d. blue ..	..	75	15
G17/18 Perf "Specimen"			*Set of* 2	£120	

*This is the date of issue for South Georgia. The stamps were placed on sale from the South Orkneys on 17 January 1947, from the South Shetlands on 30 January 1947 and from Graham Land on 10 February 1947.

1948 (6 Dec). *Royal Silver Wedding. As Nos. 166/7 of Falkland Islands, but 1s. in recess.*

G19		2½d. ultramarine	..	1·50	1·00
G20		1s. violet-blue	..	2·25	1·75

1949 (10 Oct). *75th Anniv of U.P.U. As Nos. 168/71 of Falkland Islands.*

G22		2d. carmine-red	..	5·00	2·50
G23		3d. deep blue ..	..	4·00	1·25
G24		6d. red-orange	..	7·00	3·00
G21/4		.. ..	*Set of* 4	16·00	7·50

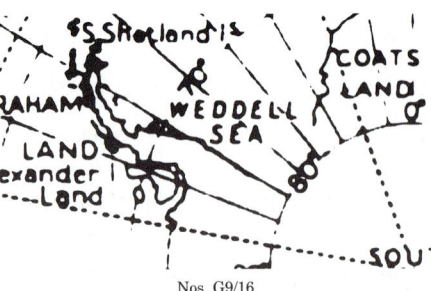
Nos. G9/16

1953 (4 June). *Coronation. As No. 186 of Falkland Islands.*

G25		1d. black and violet ..	..	1·10	1·25

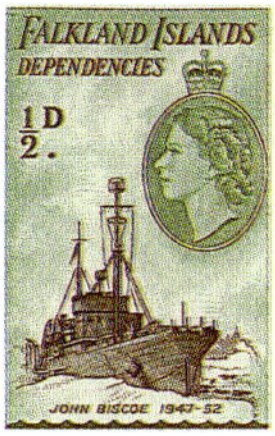

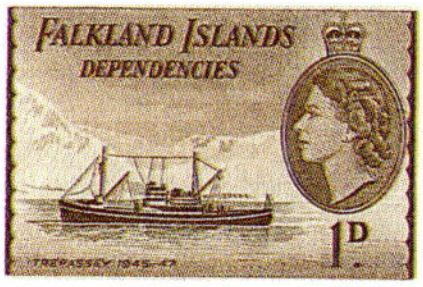

G 2 *John Biscoe I*, 1947–52   G 3 *Trepassey*, 1945–47

(Recess Waterlow, then D.L.R. (from 27.3.62))

1954 (1 Feb)–**62**. *Types* G **2/3** *and similar designs showing ships. Wmk Mult Script CA. P* 12½.

G26	½d. black and bluish green		30	2·00
	a. Black and deep green (DLR) (17.4.62)		5·50	13·00
G27	1d. black and sepia-brown		1·75	1·50
	a. Black and sepia (DLR) (27.3.62)		14·00	18·00
G28	1½d. black and olive		2·00	1·50
	a. Black and yellow-olive (DLR) (21.9.62)		8·50	3·00
G29	2d. black and rose-red		1·25	20
G30	2½d. black and yellow-ochre		1·25	15
G31	3d. black and deep bright blue		1·25	15
G32	4d. black and bright reddish purple		3·25	55
G33	6d. black and deep lilac		3·50	55
G34	9d. black		3·50	1·25
G35	1s. black and brown		3·50	1·00
G36	2s. black and carmine		19·00	10·00
G37	2s. 6d. black and pale turquoise		20·00	6·00
G38	5s. black and violet		42·00	6·50
G39	10s. black and blue		55·00	18·00
G40	£1 black		90·00	48·00
G26/40		*Set of* 15	£200	85·00

Designs: *Horiz*—1½d. *Wyatt Earp*, 1934–36; 2d. *Eagle*, 1944 45; 2½d. *Penola*, 1934–37; 3d. *Discovery II*, 1929–37; 4d. *William Scoresby*, 1926–46; 1s. *Deutschland*, 1910–12; 2s. *Pourquoi-pas?*, 1908–10; 10s. *Antarctic*, 1901–03. *Vert*—6d. *Discovery*, 1925–27; 9d. *Endurance*, 1914–16; 2s. 6d. *Français*, 1903–05; 5s. *Scotia*, 1902–04; £1 *Belgica*, 1897–99.

TRANS-ANTARCTIC EXPEDITION 1955-1958

(G 4)

1956 (30 Jan). *Trans-Antarctic Expedition. Nos.* G27, G30/1 *and* G33 *optd with Type* G **4**.

G41	1d. black and sepia-brown		10	30
G42	2½d. black and yellow-ochre		65	50
G43	3d. black and deep bright blue		65	30
G44	6d. black and deep lilac		65	30
G41/4		*Set of* 4	1·75	1·25

The stamps of Falkland Islands Dependencies were withdrawn on 16 July 1963 after Coats Land, Graham Land, South Orkneys and South Shetlands had become a separate colony, known as British Antarctic Territory.

F. SOUTH GEORGIA

From 17 July 1963 South Georgia and South Sandwich Islands used stamps inscribed "South Georgia".

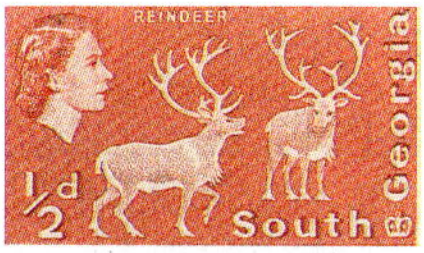

1 Reindeer

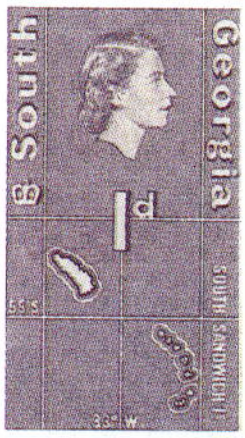

2 South Sandwich Islands

(Des D.L.R. (No. 16), M. Goaman (others). Recess D.L.R.)

1963 (17 July)–**69.** *T* **1/2** *and similar designs. Ordinary or glazed paper* (*No.* 16). *W* w **12**. *P* 15.

1	½d. brown-red		50	75
	a. Perf 14 × 15 (13.2.67)		1·00	1·50
2	1d. violet-blue		70	60
3	2d. turquoise-blue		1·25	60
4	2½d. black		5·00	2·50
5	3d. bistre		2·75	30
6	4d. bronze-green		5·00	80
7	5½d. deep violet		2·50	30
8	6d. orange		75	30
9	9d. blue		5·00	2·00
10	1s. purple		75	30
11	2s. yellow-olive and light blue		19·00	4·50
12	2s. 6d. blue		22·00	4·00
13	5s. orange-brown		22·00	4·00
14	10s. magenta		42·00	10·00
15	£1 ultramarine		85·00	48·00
16	£1 grey-black (1.12.69)		10·00	16·00
1/16		*Set of* 16	£190	80·00

Designs: *Vert*—2d. Sperm Whale; 3d. South American Fur Seal; 6d. Light-mantled Sooty Albatross; 10s. Plankton and Krill; £1 (No. 16) King Penguins. *Horiz*—2½d. Chinstrap and King Penguins; 4d. Fin Whale; 5½d. Southern Elephant-Seal; 9d. *R2* (whale-catcher); 1s. Leopard Seal; 2s. Shackleton's Cross; 2s. 6d. Wandering Albatross; 5s. Southern Elephant-seal and South American Fur Seal; £1 (No. 15) Blue Whale.

1970 (22 Jan). *As No.* 1, *but wmk* w **12** *sideways and on glazed paper.*

17	½d. brown-red	2·50	2·25

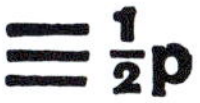

(3)

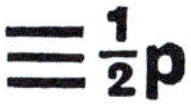

(3*a*)

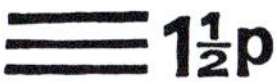

(4)

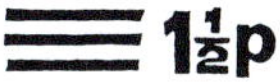

(4*a*)

(5)

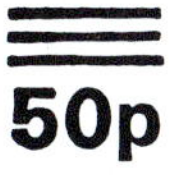

(5*a*)

1971 (15 Feb)–**76.** *Decimal Currency. Nos.* 17 *and* 2/14 *surch as T* **3/4**. *Nos.* 18/a *wmk sideways, glazed paper. Others wmk upright, ordinary paper.*

18	½p. on ½d. brown-red (T 3)		1·50	1·60
	a. Surch with T 3*a* (16.6.72)		1·00	90
	b. Do. Wmk upright (24.8.73)		3·25	5·00
19	1p. on 1d. violet-blue		1·50	55
	a. Glazed paper (1.12.72)		2·25	1·50
	b. Do. but wmk sideways (9.3.76)		1·00	4·00
20	1½p. on 5½d. deep violet (T 4)		3·00	2·25
	b. Surch with T 4*a*. Glazed paper (24.8.73)		7·00	4·50
21	2p. on 2d. turquoise-blue		70	50
22	2½p. on 2½d. black		1·50	40
23	3p. on 3d. bistre		1·00	50
24	4p. on 4d. bronze-green		90	50
25	5p. on 6d. orange		90	30
26	6p. on 9d. blue		1·50	70
27	7½p. on 1s. purple		2·00	70
28	10p. on 2s. yellow-olive and light blue		32·00	15·00
29	15p. on 2s. 6d. blue		13·00	11·00
30	25p. on 5s. orange-brown		10·00	9·00
31	50p. on 10s. magenta (Type 5)		35·00	16·00
	a. Surch with Type 5*a*. Glazed paper (1.12.72)		10·00	21·00
	b. Do. but wmk sideways (9.3.76)		15·00	32·00
18/31a		*Set of* 14	70·00	50·00

The surcharge on No. 19b shows a larger "p".
See also Nos. 53/66.

34 — Falkland Islands Dependencies   1972

6 *Endurance* beset in Weddell Sea

(Des R. Granger Barrett. Litho A. & M.)

1972 (5 Jan). *50th Death Anniv of Sir Ernest Shackleton. T* **6** *and similar horiz designs. Multicoloured. W w* **12** *(sideways*). P* 13½.

32	1½p. Type **6**	..	1·00	1·50
	w. Wmk Crown to right of CA		3·50	
33	5p. Launching the longboat *James Caird*		1·25	2·00
	w. Wmk Crown to right of CA		4·00	
34	10p. Route of the *James Caird*		1·75	2·25
	w. Wmk Crown to right of CA		4·25	
35	20p. Sir Ernest Shackleton and the *Quest*		2·00	2·50
	w. Wmk Crown to right of CA		4·50	
32/5		Set of 4	5·50	7·50

*The normal sideways watermark shows Crown to left of CA, as seen from the back of the stamp.

7 Southern Elephant-Seal and King Penguins

(Des (from photograph by D. Groves) and photo Harrison)

1972 (20 Nov). *Royal Silver Wedding. Multicoloured; background colour given. W w* **12**. *P* 14 × 14½.

36	**7**	5p. slate-green	..	75	35
		w. Wmk inverted	..	55·00	
37		10p. bluish violet	..	75	35

1973 (1 Dec*). *Royal Wedding. As Nos. 291/2 of Falkland Islands. Centre multicoloured. W w* **12** *(sideways). P* 13½.

38	5p. brown-ochre	..	25	10
39	15p. chalky blue	..	35	20

*This is the local date of issue: the Crown Agents released the stamps on 14 November.

8 Churchill and Westminster Skyline **9** Captain Cook

(Des L. Curtis. Litho Questa)

1974 (14 Dec*). *Birth Centenary of Sir Winston Churchill. T* **8** *and similar horiz design. Multicoloured. W w* **12** *(sideways). P* 14½.

40	15p. Type **8**	..	1·50	1·25
41	25p. Churchill and warship	..	1·50	1·25
MS42	122 × 98 mm. Nos. 40/1	..	6·00	6·00

*This is the local date of issue: the Crown Agents released the stamps on 30 November.

(Des J. Cooter. Litho Questa)

1975 (26 Apr). *Bicentenary of Possession by Captain Cook. T* **9** *and similar horiz designs. Multicoloured. W w* **12** *(sideways on 8 and 16p.). P* 13.

43	2p. Type **9**	..	2·25	1·25
44	8p. H.M.S. *Resolution*	..	3·50	2·00
45	16p. Possession Bay	..	3·75	2·25
43/5		Set of 3	8·50	5·00

10 *Discovery* and Biological Laboratory **11** Queen and Retinue after Coronation

(Des J. W. Litho Format)

1976 (21 Dec). *50th Anniv of "Discovery" Investigations. T* **10** *and similar vert designs. Multicoloured. W w* **14**. *P* 14.

46	2p. Type **10**	..	1·50	45
47	8p. *William Scoresby* and water-sampling bottles	..	1·75	60
48	11p. *Discovery II* and plankton net	..	2·00	65
49	25p. Biological Station and krill	..	2·50	95
46/9		Set of 4	7·00	2·40

(Des G. Drummond. Litho Questa)

1977 (7 Feb). *Silver Jubilee. T* **11** *and similar horiz designs. Multicoloured. W w* **14** *(sideways*). P* 13½.

50	6p. Visit by Prince Philip, 1957	..	50	30
51	11p. Queen Elizabeth and Westminster Abbey	..	70	35
	w. Wmk Crown to right of CA		80·00	
52	33p. Type **11**	..	80	50
50/2		Set of 3	1·75	1·00

*The normal sideways watermark shows Crown to left of CA, as seen from the back of the stamp.

1977 (17 May)–**78**. *As Nos. 18a etc., but W w* **14** *(inverted on 1p, 5p.; upright on 3p. and 50p.; sideways* on others). Glazed paper.*

53	½p. on ½d. brown-red	..	1·75	2·00
	w. Wmk Crown to right of CA		55·00	
54	1p. on 1d. violet-blue (16.8.77)	..	80	1·75
	w. Wmk upright	..	£325	
55	1½p. on 5½d. deep violet (16.8.77)	..	90	1·75
	w. Wmk Crown to right of CA		£475	
57	2½p. on 2½d. black (16.8.77)	..	12·00	3·50
58	3p. on 3d. bistre (16.8.77)	..	7·00	3·50
	w. Wmk inverted		£475	
59	4p. on 4d. bronze-green (16.8.77)	..	22·00	14·00
	w. Wmk Crown to right of CA		£650	
60	5p. on 6d. orange	..	2·50	2·75
	w. Wmk upright	..	2·50	2·75
62	7½p. on 1s. purple (16.8.77)	..	7·00	20·00
	w. Wmk Crown to right of CA (31.7.78)		1·25	8·00
63	10p. on 2s. yellow-olive & light blue (16.8.77)		5·00	9·00
	w. Wmk Crown to right of CA (31.7.78)		1·25	8·00
64	15p. on 2s. 6d. blue (16.8.77)	..	9·00	20·00
	w. Wmk Crown to right of CA (31.7.78)		2·00	8·00
65	25p. on 5s. orange-brown (16.8.77)	..	9·00	22·00
	w. Wmk Crown to right of CA (31.7.78)		1·25	8·00
66	50p. on 10s. pale magenta (12.78)	..	1·25	6·00
53/66		Set of 12	48·00	60·00

*The normal sideways watermark shows Crown to left of CA, as seen from the back of the stamp.

Surcharges on the above differ from those on Nos. 18a/30 by having straight outlines and being slightly more slender. The change in paper also results in the colours appearing brighter.

1978 Falkland Islands Dependencies — 35

12 Fur Seal

13 H.M.S. *Resolution*

(Des C. Abbott. Litho Questa)

1978 (2 June). *25th Anniv of Coronation. T* **12** *and similar vert designs. P* 15.
67	25p. indigo, ultramarine and silver	..	35	1·10
	a. Sheetlet. Nos. 67/9 × 2	..		1·75
68	25p. multicoloured	..	35	1·10
69	25p. indigo, ultramarine and silver	..	35	1·10
67/9	.. ..	Set of 3	90	3·00

Designs:—No. 67, Panther of Henry VI; No. 68, Queen Elizabeth II; No. 69, Type **12**.
Nos. 67/9 were printed together in small sheets of 6, containing two *se-tenant* strips of 3, with horizontal gutter margin between.

(Des and litho (25p. also embossed) Walsall)

1979 (14 Feb). *Bicentenary of Captain Cook's Voyages, 1768–79. T* **13** *and similar vert designs. Multicoloured. P* 11.
70	3p. Type **13**	..	1·50	1·25
71	6p. *Resolution* and map of South Georgia and S. Sandwich Isles showing route	..	1·50	1·00
72	11p. King Penguin (based on drawing by George Forster)	..	2·50	2·25
73	25p. Flaxman/Wedgwood medallion of Captain Cook	..	2·75	2·75
70/3	.. ..	Set of 4	7·50	6·50

From 5 May 1980 South Georgia and South Sandwich Islands used stamps inscribed FALKLAND ISLANDS DEPENDENCIES.

G. FALKLAND ISLANDS DEPENDENCIES

For use in South Georgia and South Sandwich Islands.

14 Map of Falkland Islands Dependencies

15 Magellanic Clubmoss

(Des and litho J.W.)

1980 (5 May)–**84**. *Horiz designs as T* **14**. *Multicoloured. W* w **14** *(sideways). P* 13½. A. Without imprint date
74A	1p. Type **14**	..	30	30
75A	2p. Shag Rocks	..	30	30
76A	3p. Bird and Willis Islands	..	30	30
77A	4p. Gulbrandsen Lake	..	30	30
78A	5p. King Edward Point	..	30	30
79A	6p. Sir Ernest Shackleton's Memorial Cross, Hope Point	..	60	30
80A	7p. Sir Ernest Shackleton's Grave, Grytviken	..	60	40
81A	8p. Grytviken Church	..	50	40
82A	9p. Coaling Hulk *Louise* at Grytviken	..	50	45
83A	10p. Clerke Rocks	..	50	45
84A	20p. Candlemas Island	..	2·75	1·75
85A	25p. Twitcher Rock and Cook Island, Southern Thule	..	2·75	1·75
86A	50p. R.R.S. *John Biscoe II* in Cumberland Bay	..	1·00	2·00
87A	£1 R.R.S. *Bransfield* in Cumberland Bay		1·25	2·75
88A	£3 H.M.S. *Endurance* in Cumberland Bay		3·00	6·50
74A/88A	.. ..	Set of 15	13·00	16·00

B. *With imprint date* ("1984") *at foot* (3.5.84)
74B	1p. Type **14**	..	25	70
75B	2p. Shag Rocks	..	25	70
76B	3p. Bird and Willis Islands	..	25	70
77B	4p. Gulbrandsen Lake	..	25	80
78B	5p. King Edward Point	..	35	80
79B	6p. Sir Ernest Shackleton's Memorial Cross, Hope Point	..	30	70
80B	7p. Sir Ernest Shackleton's Grave, Grytviken	..	30	70
81B	8p. Grytviken Church	..	30	70
82B	9p. Coaling Hulk *Louise* at Grytviken	..	30	70
83B	10p. Clerke Rocks	..	50	70
84B	20p. Candlemas Island	..	2·00	1·50
85B	25p. Twitcher Rock and Cook Island, Southern Thule	..	2·00	2·50
86B	50p. R.R.S. *John Biscoe II* in Cumberland Bay	..	2·00	2·75
74B/86B	.. ..	Set of 13	8·00	12·50

For some of these designs watermarked W **16** (sideways) see Nos. 148/52.

(Des L. McCombie. Litho Rosenbaum Bros, Vienna)

1981 (5 Feb). *Plants. T* **15** *and similar vert designs. Multicoloured. W* w **14** *(inverted on 25p.). P* 14.
89	3p. Type **15**	..	20	25
	w. Wmk inverted			7·50
90	6p. Alpine Cat's-tail	..	20	30
91	7p. Greater Burnet	..	20	30
	w. Wmk inverted			£325
92	11p. Antarctic Bedstraw	..	20	35
93	15p. Brown Rush	..	25	45
	a. Light brown (Queen's head and territory inscr) omitted			£1900
94	25p. Antarctic Hair Grass	..	35	75
	w. Wmk upright			£300
89/94	.. ..	Set of 6	1·25	2·25

16 Wedding Bouquet from Falkland Islands Dependencies

17 Introduced Reindeer during Calving, Spring

(Des J.W. Litho Format)

1981 (22 July). *Royal Wedding. T* **16** *and similar vert designs. Multicoloured. W* w **14**. *P* 14.
95	10p. Type **16**	..	15	30
96	13p. Prince Charles dressed for skiing	..	20	35
97	52p. Prince Charles and Lady Diana Spencer		65	85
95/7	.. .. ..	Set of 3	90	1·40

(Des A. Theobald. Litho Format)

1982 (29 Jan). *Reindeer. T* **17** *and similar horiz designs. Multicoloured. W* w **14** *(sideways). P* 14.
98	5p. Type **17**	..	25	65
99	13p. Bull at rut, Autumn	..	30	85
100	25p. Reindeer and mountains, Winter	..	40	1·40
101	26p. Reindeer feeding on tussock grass, late Winter	..	40	1·40
98/101	.. ..	Set of 4	1·25	3·75

36 — Falkland Islands Dependencies   1982

18 *Gamasellus racovitzai* (tick)   **19** Lady Diana Spencer at Tidworth, Hampshire, July 1981

(Des I. Loe. Litho Questa)

1982 (16 Mar). *Insects.* T **18** *and similar vert designs. Multicoloured. W w* **14**. *P* 14.
102	5p. Type **18**	.. .. ..	15	25
103	10p. *Alaskozetes antarcticus* (mite)		25	35
104	13p. *Cryptopygus antarcticus* (spring-tail)		25	40
105	15p. *Notiomaso australis* (spider) ..		30	45
106	25p. *Hydromedion sparsutum* (beetle)		50	70
107	26p. *Parochlus steinenii* (midge) ..		50	70
102/7	.. ..	Set of 6	1·75	2·50

(Des C. Abbott. Litho Format)

1982 (7 Sept). *21st Birthday of Princess of Wales.* T **19** *and similar vert designs. Multicoloured. W w* **14**. *P* 13½ × 14.
108	5p. Falklands Islands Dependencies coat of arms	..	10	15
109	17p. Type **19**		40	35
	a. Perf 13½		2·00	4·50
110	37p. Bride and groom on steps of St Paul's		45	80
111	50p. Formal portrait		1·00	1·10
108/11	.. ..	Set of 4	1·75	2·25

20 Map of South Georgia

(Des PAD Studio. Litho Format)

1982 (13 Sept). *Rebuilding Fund. W w* **14** *(sideways)*. *P* 11.
112	**20** £1 + £1 multicoloured		2·40	4·00
	w. Wmk Crown to right of CA ..		80·00	

The normal sideways watermark shows Crown to left of CA, as seen from the back of the stamp.

21 Westland Whirlwind   **22** *Euphausia superba*

(Des Harrison. Litho Questa)

1983 (23 Dec). *Bicentenary of Manned Flight.* T **21** *and similar horiz designs. Multicoloured. W w* **14** *(sideways)*. *P* 14.
113	5p. Type **21**		30	35
114	13p. Westland AS.1 Wasp helicopter	..	55	70
115	17p. Vickers Supermarine Walrus II	..	60	75
116	50p. Auster Autocrat		1·40	1·60
113/16	.. ..	Set of 4	2·50	3·00

(Des N. Weaver. Litho Questa)

1984 (23 Mar). *Crustacea.* T **22** *and similar vert designs. Multicoloured. W w* **14**. *P* 14½ × 14.
117	5p. Type **22**		40	20
118	17p. *Glyptonotus antarcticus* ..		70	50
119	25p. *Epimeria monodon*		85	60
120	34p. *Serolis pagenstecheri* ..		1·10	80
117/20	.. ..	Set of 4	2·75	1·90

23 Zavodovski Island

(Des. J.W. Litho Questa)

1984 (8 Nov). *Volcanoes of South Sandwich Islands.* T **23** *and similar horiz designs. Multicoloured. W w* **14** *(sideways)*. *P* 14 × 14½.
121	6p. Type **23**		80	80
122	17p. Mt Michael, Saunders Island	..	2·00	1·60
123	22p. Bellingshausen Island ..	..	2·00	1·75
124	52p. Bristol Island	..	2·50	3·25
121/4	.. ..	Set of 4	6·50	6·75

24 Grey-headed Albatross   **25** The Queen Mother

(Des I. Loe. Litho Questa)

1985 (5 May). *Albatrosses.* T **24** *and similar horiz designs. Multicoloured. W w* **14** *(sideways)*. *P* 14½.
125	7p. Type **25**		1·75	85
126	22p. Black-browed Albatross	..	2·50	1·40
127	27p. Wandering Albatross	..	2·75	1·60
128	54p. Light-mantled Sooty Albatross	..	3·50	2·50
125/8	.. ..	Set of 4	9·50	5·50

(Des A. Theobald (£1), C. Abbott (others). Litho Questa)

1985 (23 June). *Life and Times of Queen Elizabeth the Queen Mother.* T **25** *and similar vert designs. Multicoloured. W w* **16**. *P* 14½ × 14.
129	7p. At Windsor Castle on Princess Elizabeth's 14th birthday, 1940		30	30
130	22p. With Princess Anne, Lady Sarah Armstrong-Jones and Prince Edward at Trooping the Colour		60	70
131	27p. Type **25**		70	80
	w. Wmk inverted		10·00	
132	54p. With Prince Henry at his christening (from photo by Lord Snowdon)		1·25	1·40
129/32	.. ..	Set of 4	2·50	2·75
MS133	91 × 73 mm. £1 Disembarking from Royal Yacht *Britannia*. Wmk sideways	..	2·25	2·75

(Des I. Strange. Litho Questa)

1985 (4 Nov). *Early Naturalists. Vert designs as T* **149***a of Falkland Islands. Multicoloured. W* w **14**. *P* 14½×14.

134	7p. Dumont d'Urville and *Durvillea antarctica* (kelp)	1·25	1·00
135	22p. Johann Reinhold Forster and King Penguin	2·25	2·00
136	27p. Johann Georg Adam Forster and Tussock Grass	2·25	2·25
137	54p. Sir Joseph Banks and Dove Prion	3·00	3·50
134/7	Set of 4	8·00	8·00

1985 (18 Nov). *As Nos.* 84/8 *but W* w **16** (*sideways*). *With imprint date* ("1985"). *P* 13½.

148	20p. Candlemas Island	2·50	4·75
149	25p. Twitcher Rock and Cook Island, Southern Thule	3·00	4·75
150	50p. R.R.S. *John Biscoe* in Cumberland Bay	3·00	4·75
151	£1 R.R.S. *Bransfield* in Cumberland Bay	3·00	4·75
152	£3 H.M.S. *Endurance* in Cumberland Bay	8·00	8·00
148/52	Set of 5	17·00	24·00

Under the new constitution, effective 3 October 1985, South Georgia and South Sandwich Islands ceased to be dependencies of the Falkland Islands. Issues inscribed for the separate territory are listed under SOUTH GEORGIA AND SOUTH SANDWICH ISLANDS.

British Antarctic Territory

1963 12 pence (d) = 1 shilling
20 shillings = 1 pound
1971 100 (new) pence = 1 pound

For use at the following bases:
Adelaide Island (Graham Land) (*closed* 1977)
Argentine Islands ("Faraday" *from* 1981), (Graham Land) (*closed 8 February* 1996 *and transferred to Ukraine*)
Brabant Island (Graham Land) (*opened* 1984, *closed* 1985)
Deception Island (South Shetlands) (*closed* December 1967, *opened* 4 December 1968, *closed* 23 February 1969)
Halley Bay (Coats Land)
Hope Bay (Graham Land) (*closed* 12 February 1964)
Port Lockroy (Graham Land) (*opened* 21 November 1996)
Rothera Point (Graham Land) (*opened* 1977)
Signy Island (South Orkneys)
Stonington Island (Graham Land) (*closed* February 1975)

1 M.V. *Kista Dan*

(Des B.W. (No. 15a), M. Goaman (others). Recess B.W.)

1963 (1 Feb)–69. *Horiz designs as T* **1**, *W w* **12**. *P* 11 × 11½.
1	½d. deep blue	..	.. 90	1·40
2	1d. brown	..	.. 1·25	80
3	1½d. orange-red and brown-purple		1·25	1·25
4	2d. purple	..	.. 1·25	80
5	2½d. myrtle-green	..	.. 3·00	1·25
6	3d. deep blue	..	.. 3·75	1·25
7	4d. sepia	..	.. 2·75	1·50
8	6d. olive and deep ultramarine	..	4·50	2·00
9	9d. olive-green	..	.. 3·50	2·00
10	1s. deep turquoise-blue	..	3·75	70
11	2s. deep violet and orange-sepia		20·00	7·00
12	2s. 6d. blue	..	.. 20·00	7·50
13	5s. red-orange and rose-red	..	21·00	13·00
14	10s. deep ultramarine and emerald	..	45·00	26·00
15	£1 black and light blue	..	55·00	48·00
15a	£1 red and brownish black (1.12.69)		£150	£120
1/15a	.. .. .. Set of 16		£300	£200

Designs:—1d. Manhauling; 1½d. Muskeg (tractor); 2d. Skiing; 2½d. De Havilland D.H.C.2 Beaver (aircraft); 3d. R.R.S. *John Biscoe II*; 4d. Camp scene; 6d. H.M.S. *Protector*; 9d. Sledging; 1s. De Havilland D.H.C.3 Otter (aircraft); 2s. Huskies; 2s. 6d. Westland Whirlwind helicopter; 5s. Snocat (tractor); 10s. R.R.S. *Shackleton*; £1 (No. 15) Antarctic map; £1 (No. 15a) H.M.S. *Endurance I*.

1966 (24 Jan). *Churchill Commemoration. As Nos. 223/6 of Falkland Islands.*
16	½d. new blue	..	.. 80	3·25
17	1d. deep green	..	.. 3·00	3·25
18	1s. brown	..	.. 21·00	6·50
19	2s. bluish violet	..	24·00	7·00
16/19	.. .. .. Set of 4		45·00	18·00

17 Lemaire Channel and Icebergs

(Des R. Granger Barrett. Litho Format)

1969 (6 Feb). *25th Anniv of Continuous Scientific Work. T* **17** *and similar horiz designs. W w* **12** (*sideways*). *P* 14.
20	3½d. black, pale blue and ultramarine	..	4·00	3·00
21	6d. multicoloured	..	..	2·00	2·50
22	1s. black, pale blue and vermilion	..	2·00	2·00
23	2s. black, orange and turquoise-blue	..	2·00	3·00
20/3	.. .. .. Set of 4		9·00	9·50

Designs:—6d. Radio Sonde balloon; 1s. Muskeg pulling tent equipment; 2s. Surveyors with theodolite.

(18) **19** Setting up Camp, Graham Land

1971 (15 Feb). *Decimal Currency. As Nos. 1/14, but glazed paper, colours changed and surch as T* **18**.
24	½p. on ½d. blue	..	.. 60	3·00
25	1p. on 1d. pale brown	..	1·00	90
26	1½p. on 1½d. red and pale brown-purple		1·25	75
27	2p. on 2d. bright purple	..	1·25	40
28	2½p. on 2½d. green	..	3·00	1·75
29	3p. on 3d. blue	..	.. 2·50	75
	w. Wmk inverted		70·00	
30	4p. on 4d. bistre-brown	..	2·25	75
31	5p. on 6d. olive and ultramarine	..	4·75	3·00
32	6p. on 9d. dull green	..	16·00	8·00
33	7½p. on 1s. turquoise-blue	..	17·00	8·50
34	10p. on 2s. violet and orange-sepia		20·00	14·00
	w. Wmk inverted		£600	
35	15p. on 2s. 6d. pale blue	..	20·00	15·00
36	25p. on 5s. orange and pale rose-red		24·00	17·00
37	50p. on 10s. ultramarine and emerald	..	42·00	30·00
	w. Wmk inverted		£120	
24/37	.. .. .. Set of 14		£130	90·00

(Des M. Goaman. Recess and litho Enschedé)

1971 (23 June). *10th Anniv of Antarctic Treaty. Vert designs each including Antarctic Map and Queen Elizabeth, as T* **19**. *Multicoloured. W w* **12** (*sideways*). *P* 14 × 13.
38	1½p. Type 19	..	.. 6·00	5·50
39	4p. Snow Petrels	..	16·00	8·00
40	5p. Weddell Seals	..	9·50	8·00
41	10p. Adelie Penguins	..	22·00	9·00
38/41	.. .. .. Set of 4		48·00	27·00

PRICES OF SETS

Set prices are given for many issues, generally those containing three stamps or more. Definitive sets include one of each value or major colour change, but do not cover different perforations, die types or minor shades. Where a choice is possible the set prices are based on the cheapest versions of the stamps included in the listings.

1972   British Antarctic Territory — 39

20 Kerguelen Fur Seals and Emperor Penguins

21 James Cook and H.M.S. *Resolution*

(Des (from photograph by D. Groves) and photo Harrison)

1972 (13 Dec*). *Royal Silver Wedding. Multicoloured; background colour given.* W w **12**. P 14 × 14½.
42	**20**	5p. red-brown	3·00	3·00
		w. Wmk inverted	18·00	16·00
43		10p. brown-olive	3·00	3·00
		w. Wmk inverted	£180	

*This is the local release date; they were issued by the Crown Agents on 20 November.

(Des J.W. Litho Questa)

1973 (14 Feb*). *T* **21** *and similar vert designs. Multicoloured.* W w **12** (*sideways*). P 14 × 14½.
44	½p.	Type **21** (*shades*)	1·25	2·00
45	1p.	Thaddeus von Bellingshausen and *Vostok*	2·50	3·25
46	1½p.	James Weddell and *Jane*	11·00	4·50
47	2p.	John Biscoe and *Tula*	2·25	1·75
48	2½p.	J. S. C. Dumont d'Urville and *L'Astrolabe*	1·50	1·75
49	3p.	James Clark Ross and H.M.S. *Erebus*	95	1·75
50	4p.	C. A. Larsen and *Jason*	95	1·75
51	5p.	Adrien de Gerlache and *Belgica*	1·00	1·75
52	6p.	Otto Nordenskjöld and *Antarctic*	1·25	1·75
53	7½p.	W. S. Bruce and *Scotia*	1·50	2·25
54	10p.	Jean-Baptiste Charcot and *Pourquoi Pas?*	2·75	3·00
55	15p.	Ernest Shackleton and *Endurance*	6·00	4·00
56	25p.	Hubert Wilkins and Lockheed Vega *San Francisco*	3·00	4·00
57	50p.	Lincoln Ellsworth and Northrop Gamma *Polar Star*	2·50	4·50
58	£1	John Rymill and *Penola*	8·00	8·00
44/58		Set of 15	35·00	42·00

The 25 and 50p. show aircraft; the rest show ships. See also Nos. 64/78.

1973 (23 Dec*). *Royal Wedding. As Nos. 291/2 of Falkland Islands. Centre multicoloured.* W w **12** (*sideways*). P 13½.
59		5p. ochre	40	20
60		15p. light turquoise-blue	70	30

*This is the local date of issue: the Crown Agents released the stamps on 14 November.

22 Churchill and Churchill Peninsula, B.A.T.

(Des G. Vasarhelyi. Litho Format)

1974 (10 Dec*). *Birth Centenary of Sir Winston Churchill. T* **22** *and similar horiz design. Multicoloured.* W w **12** (*sideways on 5p.*). P 14.
61		5p. Type **22**	1·50	1·75
62		15p. Churchill and *Trepassey* ("Operation Tabarin", 1943)	1·75	2·25
MS63		114 × 88 mm. Nos. 61/2. Wmk upright	11·00	8·00

*This is the local date of issue: the Crown Agents released the stamps on 30 November.

1975 (11 June)–**81**. *As Nos. 44/58 but W w* **14**. *Ordinary paper* (½, 2, 2½, 3, 5, 10, 15, 25, 50p.) *or chalk-surfaced paper* (1, 1½, 4, 6, 7½p., £1). *P* 12 (4, 6, 7½p.) *or* 14 × 14½ (*others*).
64	½p.	Type **21**	3·00	3·25
		a. Chalk-surfaced paper (14.3.78)	75	2·50
65	1p.	Thaddeus von Bellingshausen and *Vostok* (14.3.78)	60	2·25
		a. Ordinary paper (11.12.79)	80	3·00
66	1½p.	James Weddell and *Jane* (14.3.78)	60	2·25
		a. Ordinary paper (11.12.79)	80	3·00
67	2p.	John Biscoe and *Tula* (11.12.79)	1·50	2·50
68	2½p.	J. S. C. Dumont d'Urville and *L'Astrolabe* (11.12.79)	1·50	2·50
69	3p.	James Clark Ross and H.M.S. *Erebus* (11.12.79)	2·50	2·75
70	4p.	C. A. Larsen and *Jason* (5.12.80)	55	3·00
71	5p.	Adrien de Gerlache and *Belgica* (11.12.79)	2·75	3·25
72	6p.	Otto Nordenskjöld and *Antarctic* (5.12.80)	80	3·00
73	7½p.	W. S. Bruce and *Scotia* (5.12.80)	1·25	3·50
74	10p.	Jean-Baptiste Charcot and *Pourquoi Pas?* (11.12.79)	1·75	3·25
		a. Perf 12. Chalk-surfaced paper (25.11.81)	85	3·00
75	15p.	Ernest Shackleton and *Endurance* (11.12.79)	1·25	2·00
		a. Perf 12. Chalk-surfaced paper (25.11.81)	85	3·00
76	25p.	Hubert Wilkins and Lockheed Vega *San Francisco* (11.12.79)	1·25	1·50
		a. Perf 12. Chalk-surfaced paper (25.11.81)	85	3·00
77	50p.	Lincoln Ellsworth and Northrop Gamma *Polar Star* (11.12.79)	1·25	3·00
		aw. Wmk inverted	18·00	
		b. Perf 12. Chalk-surfaced paper (5.12.80)	85	2·75
78	£1	John Rymill and *Penola* (14.3.78)	3·25	2·00
		a. Perf 12 (5.12.80)	1·50	4·00
		aw. Wmk inverted	£450	
64a/78a		Set of 15	16·00	35·00

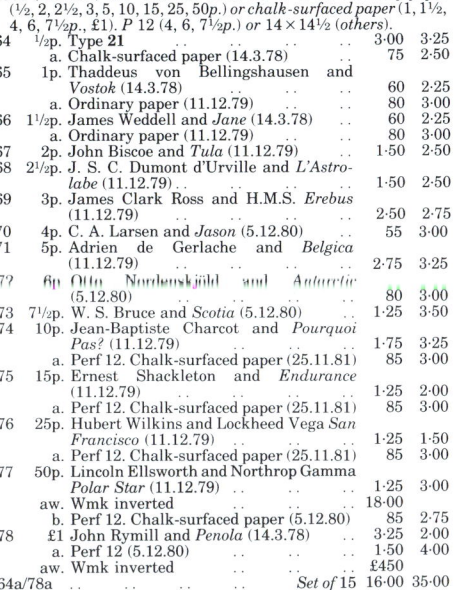

23 Sperm Whale

(Des J. Cooter. Litho Questa)

1977 (4 Jan). *Whale Conservation. T* **23** *and similar horiz designs.* W w **14** (*sideways*). P 13½.
79		2p. brownish black, slate and bright blue	6·50	4·00
80		8p. grey, brownish black and rosine	7·50	4·50
81		11p. multicoloured	8·00	4·50
82		25p. grey-blue, brownish blk & lt blue-green	8·50	6·00
79/82		Set of 4	27·00	17·00

Designs:—8p. Fin Whale; 11p. Humpback Whale; 25p. Blue Whale.

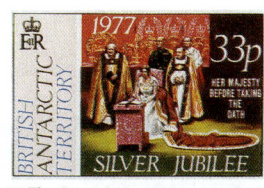

24 The Queen before Taking the Oath   **25** Emperor Penguin

40 — British Antarctic Territory — 1977

(Des J.W. Litho Questa)

1977 (7 Feb). *Silver Jubilee. T **24** and similar horiz designs. Multicoloured.* W w **14** (*sideways**). P 13½.

83	6p. Prince Philip's visit, 1956/7	.. ..	70	40
84	11p. Coronation Oath	.. ..	80	50
	w. Wmk Crown to right of CA	.. ..	6·50	7·50
85	33p. Type **24**	.. ..	1·25	65
	w. Wmk Crown to right of CA	.. ..	£160	
83/5	.. ..	*Set of* 3	2·50	1·40

*The normal sideways watermark shows Crown to left of CA, as seen from the back of the stamp.

28 Map of Antarctic

(Des C. Abbott. Litho Questa)

1978 (2 June). *25th Anniv of Coronation. T **25** and similar vert designs. P* 15.

86	25p. green, deep bluish green and silver		80	1·00
	a. Sheetlet Nos. 86/8 × 2		4·50	
87	25p. multicoloured	.. ..	80	1·00
88	25p. green, deep bluish green and silver		80	1·00
86/8	.. ..	*Set of* 3	2·25	2·75

Designs:— No. 86. Black Bull of Clarence; No. 87, Queen Elizabeth II; No. 88, Type **25**.

Nos. 86/8 were printed together in small sheets of 6, containing two *se-tenant* strips of 3 with a horizontal gutter margin between.

26 Macaroni Penguins

(Des G. Drummond. Litho Walsall)

1979 (14 Jan). *Penguins. T **26** and similar horiz designs. Multicoloured.* W w **14** (*sideways**). P 13½.

89	3p. Type **26**	.. ..	11·00	11·00
	w. Wmk Crown to right of CA	.. ..	£350	
90	8p. Gentoo penguins	.. ..	3·00	3·00
91	11p. Adelie penguins	.. ..	3·50	3·50
92	25p. Emperor penguins	.. ..	4·50	4·50
89/92	.. ..	*Set of* 4	20·00	20·00

*The normal sideways watermark shows Crown to left of CA, as seen from the back of the stamp.

27 Sir John Barrow and *Tula*

(Des A. Theobald. Litho Secura, Singapore)

1980 (14 Dec*). *150th Anniv of Royal Geographical Society. Former Presidents. T **27** and similar horiz designs. Multicoloured.* W w **14** (*sideways*†). P 13½.

93	3p. Type **27**	.. ..	20	15
94	7p. Sir Clement Markham and *Discovery*		25	25
	w. Wmk Crown to right of CA	.. ..	4·00	
95	11p. Lord Curzon and whaleboat *James Caird*		30	30
	w. Wmk Crown to right of CA	.. ..	3·00	
96	15p. Sir William Goodenough	.. ..	35	35
97	22p. Sir James Wordie	.. ..	50	55
	w. Wmk Crown to right of CA	.. ..	85·00	
98	30p. Sir Raymond Priestley	.. ..	60	65
93/8	.. ..	*Set of* 6	2·00	2·00

*This is the local date of issue; the Crown Agents released the stamps on 1 December.

†The normal sideways watermark shows Crown to left of CA, as seen from the back of the stamp.

(Des Walsall. Litho Questa)

1981 (1 Dec). *20th Anniv of Antarctic Treaty. T **28** and similar horiz designs.* W w **14** (*sideways**). P 13½×14.

99	10p. black, new blue and azure	..	40	80
	w. Wmk Crown to right of CA	..	£200	
100	13p. black, new blue and apple-green		45	90
101	25p. black, new blue and mauve	..	55	1·00
102	26p. black, brown-ochre and rose-red		55	1·00
99/102	.. ..	*Set of* 4	1·75	3·25

Designs:—13p. Conservation research ("scientific co-operation"); 25p. Satellite image mapping ("technical co-operation"); 26p Global geophysics ("scientific co-operation").

*The normal sideways watermark shows Crown to left of CA, as seen from the back of the stamp.

29 Map of Gondwana showing position of Continents 280 million years ago, and Contemporary Landscape Scene

30 British Antarctic Territory Coat of Arms

(Des C. Abbott. Litho Walsall)

1982 (8 Mar). *Gondwana—Continental Drift and Climatic Change. T **29** and similar horiz designs depicting maps of Gondwana showing position of continents, and contemporary landscape scenes. Multicoloured.* W w **14** (*sideways*). P 13½ × 14.

103	3p. Type **29**	.. ..	25	40
104	6p. 260 million years ago	.. ..	30	50
105	10p. 230 million years ago	.. ..	35	60
106	13p. 175 million years ago	.. ..	45	70
107	25p. 50 million years ago	.. ..	55	75
108	26p. Present day	.. ..	55	75
	a. Gold (royal cypher) omitted			
103/8	.. .. ..	*Set of* 6	2·25	3·25

(Des Jennifer Toombs. Litho Questa)

1982 (1 July). *21st Birthday of Princess of Wales. T **30** and similar vert designs. Multicoloured.* W w **14**. P 14½ × 14.

109	5p. Type **30**	.. ..	20	20
110	17p. Princess of Wales (detail of painting by Bryan Organ)	.. ..	45	50
111	37p. Wedding ceremony	.. ..	70	80
112	50p. Formal portrait	.. ..	1·10	1·10
109/12	.. ..	*Set of* 4	2·25	2·40

31 Leopard Seal

1983 British Antarctic Territory — 41

(Des R. Granger Barrett. Litho Walsall)

1983 (3 Jan). *10th Anniv (1982) of Antarctic Seal Conservation Convention.* T **31** *and similar horiz designs. Multicoloured.* W w 14 (*sideways*). P 11.

113	5p. Type **31**			45	35
114	10p. Weddell Seals			50	40
115	13p. Southern Elephant Seals			55	45
116	17p. Kerguelen Fur Seals			65	55
117	25p. Ross Seal			75	65
118	34p. Crabeater Seals			95	85
113/18			Set of 6	3·50	3·00

32 De Havilland D.H.C.6 Twin Otter 200/300

(Des Harrison. Litho Questa)

1983 (20 Dec). *Bicentenary of Manned Flight.* T **32** *and similar horiz designs. Multicoloured.* W w 14 (*sideways*). P 14.

119	5p. Type **32**			25	30
120	13p. De Havilland D.H.C.3 Otter			40	45
121	17p. Consolidated PBY-5A Canso			55	60
122	50p. Lockheed Vega *San Francisco*			1·10	1·25
119/22			Set of 4	2·10	2·40

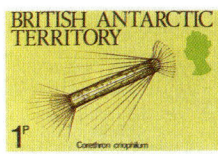

33 *Corethron criophilum*

(Des I. Loe. Litho Walsall)

1984 (15 Mar). *Marine Life.* T **33** *and similar horiz designs. Multicoloured.* W w 14 (*sideways**). P 14.

123	1p. Type **33**			60	1·40
124	2p. *Desmonema gaudichaudi*			65	1·40
125	3p. *Tomopteris carpenteri*			65	1·40
126	4p. *Pareuchaeta antarctica*			70	1·50
127	5p. *Antarctomysis maxima*			70	1·50
128	6p. *Antarcturus signiensis*			70	1·50
129	7p. *Serolis cornuta*			70	1·50
130	8p. *Parathemisto gaudichaudii*			70	1·50
131	9p. *Bovallia gigantea*			70	1·50
132	10p. *Euphausia superba*			70	1·50
133	15p. *Colossendeis australis*			70	1·75
134	20p. *Todarodes sagittatus*			75	1·75
	w. Wmk Crown to right of CA			80·00	
135	25p. Antarctic Rockcod ("*Notothenia neglecta*")			80	1·75
136	50p. Black-finned Icefish ("*Chaenocephalus aceratus*")			1·25	2·00
137	£1 Crabeater Seal			1·75	2·50
138	£3 Antarctic marine food chain			5·00	6·50
123/38			Set of 16	15·00	28·00

*The normal sideways watermark shows Crown to left of CA on 1, 3, 4, 6, 7, 8, 9, 10, 20p. and to right on 2, 5, 15, 25, 50p., £1, £3, *all as seen from the back of the stamp*.

The new-issue supplement to this Catalogue appears each month in

GIBBONS STAMP MONTHLY

—from your newsagent or by postal subscription— sample copy and details on request.

34 M.Y. *Penola* in Stella Creek   **35** Robert McCormick and McCormick's Skua

(Des A. Theobald. Litho Questa)

1985 (23 Mar). *50th Anniv of British Graham Land Expedition.* T **34** *and similar horiz designs. Multicoloured.* W w 14 (*sideways*). P 14½.

139	7p. Type **34**			40	75
140	22p. Northern Base, Winter Island			70	1·40
141	27p. De Havilland D.H.83 Fox Moth at Southern Base, Barry Island			80	1·60
142	54p. Dog team near Ablation Point, George VI Sound			1·50	2·25
139/42			Set of 4	3·00	5·50

(Des I. Strange. Litho Questa)

1985 (4 Nov). *Early Naturalists.* T **35** *and similar vert designs. Multicoloured.* W w 14. P 14½ × 14.

143	7p. Type **35**			1·25	1·50
144	22p. Sir Joseph Dalton Hooker and *Deschampsia antarctica*			1·75	2·75
145	27p. Jean René C. Quoy and Hourglass Dolphin			1·90	2·75
146	54p. James Weddell and Weddell Seal			2·75	4·00
143/6			Set of 4	7·00	10·00

 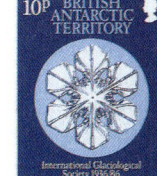

36 Dr. Edmond Halley   **37** Snow Crystal

(Des A. Theobald. Litho Questa)

1986 (6 Jan). *Appearance of Halley's Comet.* T **36** *and similar vert designs. Multicoloured.* W w 14. P 14.

147	7p. Type **36**			1·00	1·25
148	22p. Halley Station, Antarctica			1·75	2·25
149	27p. "Halley's Comet, 1531" (from Peter Apian woodcut, 1532)			2·00	2·50
150	54p. *Giotto* spacecraft			3·50	4·50
147/50			Set of 4	7·50	9·50

(Des C. Abbott. Litho Questa)

1986 (6 Dec). *50th Anniv of International Glaciological Society.* T **37** *and similar vert designs showing snow crystals.* W w 16. P 14½.

151	10p. cobalt and deep ultramarine			60	75
152	24p. pale turquoise-green & dp bluish green			90	1·40
153	29p. mauve and deep mauve			1·00	1·80
154	58p. violet-blue and bright violet			1·40	2·50
151/4			Set of 4	3·50	5·50

42 — British Antarctic Territory 1987

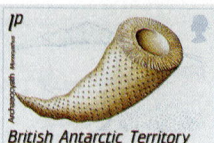

38 Captain Scott, 1904
39 I.G.Y. Logo
42 Monocyathus (archaeocyath)
43 Late Cretaceous Forest and Southern Beech Fossil

(Des A. Theobald. Litho Questa)

1987 (19 Mar). *75th Anniv of Captain Scott's Arrival at South Pole. T* **38** *and similar horiz designs. Multicoloured.* W w **16** (*sideways*). P 14 × 14½.
155	10p. Type **38**	85	95
156	24p. Hut Point and *Discovery*, Ross Island, 1902–4	1·40	2·00
157	29p. Cape Evans Hut, 1911–13	1·75	2·25
158	58p. Scott's Expedition at South Pole, 1912	2·25	3·00
155/8	Set of 4	5·50	7·50

(Des L. Curtis. Litho Questa)

1987 (25 Dec). *30th Anniv of International Geophysical Year. T* **39** *and similar vert designs.* W w **16**. P 14½ × 14.
159	10p. black and pale green	30	75
160	24p. multicoloured	60	1·40
161	29p. multicoloured	75	1·75
162	58p. multicoloured	1·40	2·50
159/62	Set of 4	2·75	5·75

Designs:—24p. Port Lockroy; 29p. Argentine Islands; 58p. Halley Bay.

40 Aurora over South Ice Plateau Station
41 *Xanthoria elegans*

(Des D. Hartley. Litho Questa)

1988 (19 Mar). *30th Anniv of Commonwealth Trans-Antarctic Expedition. T* **40** *and similar vert designs. Multicoloured.* W w **16**. P 14.
163	10p. Type **40**	30	55
164	24p. "Otter" aircraft at Theron Mountains	60	90
165	29p. Seismic ice-depth sounding	70	1·10
166	58p. "Sno-cat" over crevasse	1·25	1·75
163/6	Set of 4	2·50	3·75

(Des I. Loe. Litho Walsall)

1989 (25 Mar). *Lichens. T* **41** *and similar horiz designs. Multicoloured.* W w **14** (*sideways*). P 14.
167	10p Type **41**	90	90
168	24p *Usnea aurantiaco-atra*	1·60	1·75
169	29p *Cladonia chlorophaea*	1·75	1·90
170	58p *Umbilicaria antarctica*	2·50	3·25
167/70	Set of 4	6·00	7·00

(Des I. Loe. Litho Questa)

1990 (2 Apr). *Fossils. T* **42** *and similar horiz designs. Multicoloured.* W w **16** (*sideways*). P 14.
171	1p. Type **42**	75	1·00
172	2p. *Lingulella* (brachiopod)	75	1·00
173	3p. *Triplagnoslus* (trilobite)	90	1·00
174	4p. *Lyriaspis* (trilobite)	90	1·00
175	5p. *Glossopteris* leaf (gymnosperm)	90	1·00
176	6p. *Gonatosorus* (fern)	1·00	1·10
177	7p. *Belemnopsis aucklandica* (belemnite)	1·00	1·10
178	8p. *Sanmartinoceras africanum insignicostatum* (ammonite)	1·00	1·10
179	9p. *Pinna antarctica* (mussel)	1·00	1·10
180	10p. *Aucellina andina* (mussel)	1·00	1·10
181	20p. *Pterotrigonia malagninoi* (mussel)	1·50	1·60
182	25p. *Anchura* sp. (conch shell)	1·50	1·60
183	50p. *Ainoceras zinsmeisteri* (ammonite)	2·00	2·75
184	£1 *Gunnarites antarcticus* (ammonite)	3·50	4·25
185	£3 *Hoploparia* (crayfish)	7·00	8·00
171/85	Set of 15	22·00	26·00

(Des D. Miller. Litho Questa)

1990 (25 Dec*). *90th Birthday of Queen Elizabeth the Queen Mother. Vert designs as T* **165a** (26p.) *or* **165b** (£1) *of Falkland Islands.* W w **16**. P 14×15 (26p.) *or* 14½ (£1).
186	26p. multicoloured	1·75	2·25
187	£1 brownish black and olive-bistre	3·75	4·25

Designs:—26p. Wedding of Prince Albert and Lady Elizabeth Bowes-Lyon, 1923; £1 The Royal Family, 1940.

*This is the local date of issue, the Crown Agents released the stamps on 4 August.

(Des N. Shewring. Litho Questa)

1991 (27 Mar). *Age of the Dinosaurs. T* **43** *and similar horiz designs. Multicoloured.* W w **14** (*sideways*). P 14×13½.
188	12p. Type **43**	1·25	1·25
189	26p. Hypsilophodont dinosaurs and skull	2·00	2·25
190	31p. Frilled Sharks and tooth	2·25	2·50
191	62p. Mosasaur, Plesiosaur, and Mosasaur vertebra	3·50	4·00
188/91	Set of 4	8·00	9·00

44 Launching Meteorological Balloon, Halley IV Station
45 Researching Dry Valley

(Des O. Bell. Litho Questa)

1991 (30 Mar). *Discovery of Antarctic Ozone Hole. T* **44** *and similar horiz designs. Multicoloured.* W w **16** (*sideways*). P 14×13½.
192	12p. Type **44**	90	90
193	26p. Measuring ozone with Dobson spectrophotometer	1·60	1·75

1991 British Antarctic Territory — 43

194	31p.	Satellite map showing ozone hole	..	1·75	1·90
195	62p.	Lockheed ER-2 aircraft and graph of chlorine monoxide and ozone levels		3·00	3·25
192/5	..	.. .. ..	Set of 4	6·50	7·00

(Des O. Bell. Litho Questa)

1991 (2 Dec*). *30th Anniv of Antarctic Treaty*. T **45** *and similar vert designs*. W w **14**. P 13½×14 (31p.) or 14½×14 (*others*).

196	12p.	multicoloured	.. ..	90	90
197	26p.	multicoloured	..	1·60	1·75
198	31p.	black and blue-green	..	1·75	1·90
199	62p.	multicoloured	..	3·00	3·25
196/9	..	.. .. ..	Set of 4	6·50	7·00

Designs:—26p. Relief map of ice sheet; 31p. BIOMASS logo; 62p. Ross Seal.
*This is the local date of issue, the Crown Agents released the stamps on 24 June.

46 "H.M.S. *Erebus* and H.M.S. *Terror* in the Antarctic" (J. Carmichael)

(Des R. Watton. Litho Walsall)

1991 (10 Dec). *Maiden Voyage of James Clark Ross (research ship)*. T **46** *and similar horiz designs. Multicoloured*. W w **14** (*sideways*). P 14½.

200	12p.	Type **46**	.. ..	90	90
201	26p.	Launch of *James Clark Ross*		1·60	1·75
202	31p.	*James Clark Ross* in Antarctica	..	1·75	1·90
203	62p.	Scientific research	..	3·00	3·25
200/3	..	.. .. ..	Set of 4	6·50	7·00

1991 (24 Dec). *Birth Bicentenary of Michael Faraday (scientist)*. Nos. 200/3 *additionally inscr* "200th Anniversary M. Faraday 1791–1867" *in blue*.

204	12p.	Type **46**	.. ..	90	90
205	26p.	Launch of *James Clark Ross*		1·60	1·75
206	31p.	*James Clark Ross* in Antarctica	..	1·75	1·90
207	62p.	Scientific research	..	3·00	3·25
204/7	..	.. .. ..	Set of 4	6·50	7·00

47 Ross Seals

(Des A. Robinson. Litho B.D.T.)

1992 (10 Dec*). *Endangered Species. Seals and Penguins*. T **47** *and similar horiz designs. Multicoloured*. W w **14** (*sideways*). P 13½.

208	4p.	Type **47**	.. .. ..	80	80
209	5p.	Adelie Penguins	..	80	80
210	7p.	Weddell Seal with pup	..	85	85
211	29p.	Emperor Penguins with chicks		2·00	2·00
212	34p.	Crabeater Seals with pup	..	1·75	2·00
213	68p.	Chinstrap Penguins with young		2·25	2·40
208/13	..	.. ..	Set of 6	7·50	8·00

*This is the local date of issue, the Crown Agents released the stamps in London, and at the "Genova 92" International Thematic Stamp Exhibition, on 20 October.
Nos. 212/13 do not carry the W.W.F. Panda emblem.

48 Sun Pillar at Faraday 49 *Fitzroy* (mail and supply ship)

(Des N. Shewring. Litho Questa)

1992 (22 Dec). *Lower Atmospheric Phenomena*. T **48** *and similar horiz designs. Multicoloured*. W w **14** (*sideways*). P 14½.

214	14p.	Type **48**	.. .. ..	80	70
215	29p.	Halo over iceberg	.. ..	1·40	1·00
216	34p.	Lee Wave Cloud	.. ..	1·75	1·25
217	68p.	Nacreous Clouds	.. ..	2·75	2·00
214/17	..	.. ..	Set of 4	6·00	4·50

(Des R. Watton. Litho Walsall)

1993 (13 Dec). *Antarctic Ships*. T **49** *and simlar horiz designs. Multicoloured*. W w **14** (*sideways*). P 14.

218	1p.	Type **49**	.. ..	35	50
219	2p.	*William Scoresby* (research ship)	..	40	50
220	3p.	*Eagle* (sealer)		45	50
221	4p.	*Trepassey* (supply ship)	..	45	50
222	5p.	*John Biscoe I* (research ship)		45	50
223	10p.	*Norsel* (supply ship)	..	60	70
224	20p.	H.M.S. *Protector* (ice patrol ship)		90	70
225	30p.	*Oluf Sven* (supply ship)	..	1·10	1·25
226	50p.	*John Biscoe II* and *Shackleton* (research ships)		1·60	1·60
227	£1	*Tottan* (supply ship)	..	2·50	2·75
228	£3	*Perla Dan* (supply ship)		6·00	6·50
229	£5	H.M.S. *Endurance I* (ice patrol ship)		10·00	11·00
218/29	..	..	Set of 12	22·00	24·00

For miniature sheets containing the 50p or £1 ("1997" imprint date) see Nos. **MS**274/5.

1994 (19 Mar*). "*Hong Kong '94" International Stamp Exhibition*. Nos. 240/5 *optd as* T **178***a of Falkland Islands*.

230	15p.	Type **51**	.. .. ..	85	1·00
231	24p.	De Havilland D.H.C.2 Turbo Beaver III aircraft		1·25	1·75
232	31p.	De Havilland D.H.C.3 Otter aircraft and dog team		1·50	1·90
233	36p.	De Havilland D.H.C.6 Twin Otter 200/300 aircraft and dog team	..	1·60	2·00
234	62p.	De Havilland D.H.C.7 Dash Seven aircraft over landing strip, Rothera Point	..	2·25	2·75
235	72p.	De Havilland D.H.C.7 Dash Seven aircraft on runway	..	2·25	2·75
230/5	..	..	Set of 6	8·75	11·00

*This is the local release date, the Crown Agents released the stamps in London and at the Exhibition on 18 February.

50 Bransfield House Post Office, Port Lockroy

44 — British Antarctic Territory 1994

(Des R. Watton. Litho Walsall)

1994 (19 Mar). *50th Anniv of Operation Tabarin. T* **50** *and similar horiz designs. Multicoloured. W* w **16** *(sideways). P* 14×14½.

236	15p. Type **50**		65	75
237	31p. Survey team, Hope Bay		1·10	1·25
238	36p. Dog team, Hope Bay		1·40	1·60
239	72p. Fitzroy (supply ship) and H.M.S. William Scoresby (minesweeper)		2·25	2·75
236/9		Set of 4	4·75	5·50

51 Huskies and Sledge

(Des D. Miller. Litho Walsall)

1994 (21 Mar). *Forms of Transportation. T* **51** *and similar horiz designs. Multicoloured. W* w **14** *(sideways). P* 14½.

240	15p. Type **51**		60	70
241	24p. De Havilland D.H.C.2 Turbo Beaver III aircraft		80	90
242	31p. De Havilland D.H.C.3 Otter aircraft and dog team		90	1·00
243	36p. De Havilland D.H.C.6 Twin Otter 200/300 aircraft and dog team		1·00	1·25
244	62p. De Havilland D.H.C.7 Dash Seven aircraft over landing strip, Rothera Point		1·90	2·50
245	72p. De Havilland D.H.C.7 Dash Seven aircraft on runway		2·00	2·75
240/5		Set of 6	6·50	8·00

52 Capt. James Cook and H.M.S. *Resolution*

(Des R. Watton. Litho Questa)

1994 (23 Nov). *Antarctic Heritage Fund. T* **52** *and similar horiz designs. Multicoloured. W* w **16** *(sideways). P* 14½×14.

246	17p. + 3p. Type **52**		1·50	1·60
247	35p. + 15p. Sir James Clark Ross with H.M.S. *Erebus* and H.M.S. *Terror*		1·75	1·90
248	40p. + 10p. Capt. Robert Falcon Scott and interior of hut		1·75	1·90
249	76p. + 4p. Sir Ernest Shackleton and *Endurance*		2·50	2·75
246/9		Set of 4	6·75	7·25

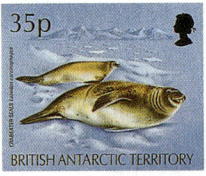

53 Pair of Crabeater Seals

54 Hauberg Mountains

(Des A. Robinson. Litho Questa)

1994 (29 Nov). *Antarctic Food Chain. T* **53** *and similar horiz designs. Multicoloured. W* w **14**. *P* 14×14½.

250	35p. Type **53**		1·25	1·50
	a. Sheetlet. Nos. 250/5		6·50	
251	35p. Blue Whale		1·25	1·50
252	35p. Wandering Albatross		1·25	1·50
253	35p. Mackerel Icefish		1·25	1·50
254	35p. Krill		1·25	1·50
255	35p. Seven Star Flying Squid (*Martialia hyadesi*)		1·25	1·50
250/5		Set of 6	6·50	8·00

Nos. 250/5 were printed together, *se-tenant*, in sheetlets of 6.

(Des N. Shewring. Litho Walsall)

1995 (28 Nov). *Geological Structures. T* **54** *and similar horiz designs. Multicoloured. W* w **14** *(sideways). P* 14×14½.

256	17p. Type **54**		75	75
257	35p. Arrowsmith Peninsula		1·50	1·50
258	40p. Colbert Mountains		1·75	1·75
259	76p. Succession Cliffs		2·50	2·50
256/9		Set of 4	6·00	6·00

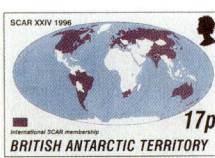

55 World Map showing Member Countries

(Des R. Watton. Litho Walsall)

1996 (23 Mar). *24th Meeting of Scientific Committee on Antarctic Research, Cambridge. T* **55** *and similar horiz designs. Multicoloured. W* w **16** *(sideways). P* 14.

260	17p. Type **55**		75	75
261	35p. Scientist analysing ice samples		1·50	1·50
262	40p. Releasing balloon		1·75	1·75
263	76p. Antarctic research ship catching marine life		2·50	2·50
260/3		Set of 4	6·00	6·00
MS264	100×90 mm. £1 S.C.A.R. logo. Wmk inverted		3·50	4·00

56 Killer Whales

57 Chinstrap Penguins sledging

(Des Dafila Scott. Litho Questa)

1996 (25 Nov). *Whales. T* **56** *and similar horiz designs. Multicoloured. W* w **14** *(sideways). P* 14.

265	17p. Type **56**		70	60
266	35p. Sperm Whales		1·25	1·10
267	40p. Minke Whales		1·50	1·40
268	76p. Blue Whale and calf		2·25	2·00
265/8		Set of 4	5·00	4·50
MS269	105×82 mm. £1 Humpback Whale		2·50	2·75

(Des D. Miller. Litho Walsall)

1996 (25 Nov). *70th Birthday of Queen Elizabeth II. Vert designs as T* **188***a of Falkland Islands, each incorporating a different photograph of the Queen. Multicoloured. W* w **16**. *P* 14½.

270	17p. At premiere of *Chaplin*, Leicester Square, 1992		50	60
271	35p. At Buckingham Palace dinner, 1991		95	1·25
272	40p. In Aberdeen, 1993		1·25	1·50
273	76p. At Royal Military School of Music, 1990		1·75	2·25
270/3		Set of 4	4·00	5·00

1997 British Antarctic Territory — 45

(Des D. Miller. Litho Questa)

1997 (3 Feb). *"HONG KONG '97" International Stamp Exhibition. Sheet 130×90 mm, containing design as No. 226. Multicoloured. W w* **14**. *P* 14.
MS274 50p. *John Biscoe II* and *Shackleton* (research ships) .. .. .. 1·40 1·40

(Des R. Watton. Litho Walsall)

1997 (20 June). *Return of Hong Kong to China. Sheet 130×90 mm containing design as No. 227, but with "1997" imprint date.*
MS275 £1 *Tottan* .. .. .. 2·75 3·00

(Des R. Watton. Litho Questa)

1997 (22 Dec). *Christmas. T* **57** *and similar vert designs. Multicoloured. W w* **16**. *P* 14½×14.
276 17p. Type **57** 75 75
277 35p. Emperor Penguins carol singing .. 1·40 1·40
278 40p. Adelié Penguins throwing snowballs 1·60 1·60
279 76p. Gentoo Penguins ice-skating .. 2·25 2·75
276/9 .. .. .. *Set of* 4 5·50 6·00

(Des D. Miller. Litho Questa)

1998 (17 Mar). *Diana, Princess of Wales Commemoration. Sheet, 145×70 mm, containing vert designs as T* **196**a *of Falkland Islands. Multicoloured. W w* **14** (*sideways*). *P* 14½×14.
MS280 35p. Wearing sunglasses; 35p. Wearing round-necked white blouse, 1993; 35p. Wearing white blouse and jacket, 1990; 35p. Wearing green jacket, 1992 (*sold at* £1.40 + 20p. *charity premium*) .. .. 3·75 3·75

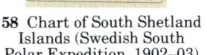

58 Chart of South Shetland Islands (Swedish South Polar Expedition, 1902–03)

59 Antarctic Explorer and H.M.S. *Erebus*, 1843

(Des N. Shewring. Litho Walsall)

1998 (19 Mar). *History of Mapping in Antarctica. T* **58** *and similar vert designs. Multicoloured. W w* **14**. *P* 14.
281 16p. Type **58** 75 75
282 30p. Map of Antarctic Peninsula (1949) .. 1·25 1·25
283 35p. Map of Antarctic Peninsula (1964) .. 1·40 1·40
284 40p. Map of Antarctic Peninsula from Landsat (1981) .. .. 1·50 1·50
285 65p. Map of Antarctic Peninsula from satellite (1995) .. .. 1·75 2·25
281/5 .. .. .. *Set of* 5 6·00 6·50

(Des V. Ambrus. Litho Walsall)

1998 (27 Nov). *Antarctic Clothing. T* **59** *and similar vert designs. Multicoloured. W w* **14**. *P* 14½×14.
286 30p. Type **59** 80 80
287 35p. Explorer with dog and *Discovery I*, 1900 .. .. .. 90 90
288 40p. Surveyor and *Fitzroy*, 1943 .. 1·10 1·10
289 65p. Scientist with penguins and *James Clark Ross*, 1998 .. .. 1·60 1·60
286/9 .. .. .. *Set of* 4 4·00 4·00

60 Snowy Sheathbill

(Des A. Robinson. Litho Walsall)

1998 (30 Nov). *Antarctic Birds. T* **60** *and similar horiz designs. Multicoloured. W w* **14** (*sideways*). *P* 14.
290 1p. Type **60** 10 10
291 2p. Dove Prion ("Antarctic Prion") .. 10 10
292 5p. Adelié Penguin 10 10
293 10p. Emperor Penguin 20 25
294 20p. Swallow-tailed Tern ("Antarctic Tern") 40 45
295 30p. Black-bellied Storm Petrel .. 60 65
296 35p. Antarctic Fulmar 70 75
297 40p. Blue-eyed Shag 80 85
298 50p. McCormick's Skua .. .. 1·00 1·10
299 £1 Southern Black-backed Gull ("Kelp Gull") .. .. 2·00 2·10
300 £3 Wilson's Storm Petrel .. 6·00 6·25
301 £5 Brown Skua .. .. 10·00 10·50
290/301 .. .. *Set of* 12 21·00 22·00

61 Mackerel Icefish

(Des C. Austin. Litho Cartor)

1999 (14 Nov). *Fish of the Southern Ocean. T* **61** *and similar horiz designs. Multicoloured. W w* **14**. *P* 13½.
302 10p. Type **61** 20 25
303 20p. Blenny Rockcod ("Toothfish") .. 40 45
304 25p. Borch 50 55
305 50p. Marbled Rockcod ("Marbled notothen") 1·00 1·10
306 80p. Bernacchi's Rockcod ("Bernach") 1·60 1·75
302/6 .. .. .. *Set of* 6 3·50 4·00

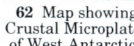

62 Map showing Crustal Microplates of West Antarctica

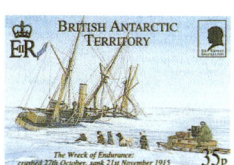

63 Wreck of *Endurance*

(Des N. Shewring. Litho Questa)

1999 (18 Dec). *British Antarctic Survey Discoveries. T* **62** *and similar multicoloured designs. W w* **14** (*sideways on horiz designs*). *P* 14.
307 15p. Type **62** 30 35
308 30p. Testing lead levels in ice .. 60 65
309 35p. Decolopodid sea spider (Gigantism in marine invertebrates) (*horiz*) .. 70 75
310 40p. Scientist operating Dobson Spectrophotometer for testing ozone layer (*horiz*) 80 85
311 70p. Radar antenna (aurora electric field research) (*horiz*) .. .. 1·40 1·50
307/11 .. .. *Set of* 5 3·75 4·00

(Des M. Skidmore. Litho Questa)

2000 (10 Feb). *Shackleton's Trans-Antarctic Expedition, 1914–17, Commemoration.* T **63** *and similar horiz designs. Multicoloured.* W w **14** *(sideways). P 14.*

312	35p. Type **63**	70	75
313	40p. Ocean Camp on ice	80	85
314	65p. Launching *James Caird* from Elephant Island	1·25	1·40
312/14	Set of 3	2·75	3·00

(Des R. Hutchins. Litho Cartor)

2000 (23 May). *"Heroic Age of Antarctica". Commonwealth Trans-Antarctic Expedition, 1955–58.* T **64** *and similar horiz designs. Multicoloured.* W w **14** *(sideways). P 13½.*

315	37p. Type **64**	75	80
	a. Sheetlet. Nos. 315/20	4·50	
316	37p. Expedition at South Pole, 1958	75	80
317	37p. *Magga Dan* (Antarctic supply ship)	75	80
318	37p. Sno-cat repair camp	75	80
319	37p. Sno-cat over crevasse	75	80
320	37p. Seismic explosion	75	80
315/20	Set of 6	4·50	4·75

Nos. 315/20 were printed together, *se-tenant*, in sheetlets of 6 with enlarged illustrated right and bottom margins.

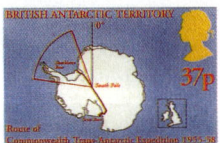

64 Route of Commonwealth Trans-Antarctic Expedition, 1955–58

South Georgia and the South Sandwich Islands

100 (new) pence = 1 pound

As South Georgia was a dependency of the Falkland Islands between 1963 and 1980 stamps so inscribed are listed under FALKLAND ISLANDS DEPENDENCIES.

Under the new constitution, effective 3 October 1985, South Georgia and South Sandwich Islands ceased to be dependencies of the Falkland Islands.

(Des A. Theobald. Litho Questa)

1986 (21 Apr). 60th Birthday of Queen Elizabeth II. Vert designs as T **150a** of Falkland Islands. Multicoloured. W w **16**. P 14½×14.

153	10p.	Four generations of Royal Family at Prince Charles' christening, 1948	35	35
154	24p.	With Prince Charles and Lady Diana Spencer, Buckingham Palace, 1981	60	65
155	29p.	In robes of Order of the British Empire, St. Paul's Cathedral, London	60	70
156	45p.	At banquet, Canada, 1976	80	95
157	58p.	At Crown Agents Head Office, London, 1983	1·00	1·25
153/7		Set of 5	3·00	3·50

26a I.G.Y. Logo

27 *Gaimardia trapesina*

(Des L. Curtis. Litho Questa)

1987 (5 Dec). 30th Anniv of International Geophysical Year. T **26**a and similar vert designs. W w **16**. P 14½×14.

176	24p.	black and pale turquoise-blue	70	55
177	29p.	multicoloured	75	60
178	58p.	multicoloured	1·40	1·25
176/8		Set of 3	2·50	2·10

Designs:—29p. Grytviken; 58p. Glaciologist using hand-drill to take core sample.

25a Prince Andrew and Miss Sarah Ferguson at Ascot

26 Southern Black-backed Gull

(Des D. Miller. Litho Questa)

1986 (10 Nov). Royal Wedding. T **25a** and similar vert designs. Multicoloured. W w **16**. P 14½×14.

158	17p.	Type **25a**	75	1·10
159	22p.	Wedding photograph	85	1·25
160	29p.	Prince Andrew with Westland WG-13 Lynx helicopter on board H.M.S. Brazen	1·50	1·50
158/60		Set of 3	2·75	3·50

(Des T. Chater. Litho Walsall)

1987 (24 Apr). Birds. T **26** and similar multicoloured designs. W w **16** (sideways on horiz designs). P 14½.

161	1p.	Type **26**	55	90
162	2p.	Blue-eyed Cormorant	65	1·00
163	3p.	Snowy Sheathbill (*vert*)	80	1·25
		w. Wmk inverted	£200	
164	4p.	Great Skua (*vert*)	65	1·25
165	5p.	Pintado Petrel ("Cape Pigeon")	65	1·25
166	6p.	Georgian Diving Petrel	65	1·25
167	7p.	South Georgia Pipit (*vert*)	75	1·40
168	8p.	Georgian Teal ("South Georgian Pintail") (*vert*)	75	1·40
169	9p.	Fairy Prion	75	1·40
170	10p.	Chinstrap Penguin	1·00	1·40
171	20p.	Macaroni Penguin (*vert*)	1·25	1·75
172	25p.	Light-mantled Sooty Albatross (*vert*)	1·25	1·75
		w. Wmk inverted	£400	
173	50p.	Giant Petrel (*vert*)	1·75	2·25
174	£1	Wandering Albatross	2·25	3·50
175	£3	King Penguin (*vert*)	6·00	7·50
161/75		Set of 15	18·00	26·00

(Des I. Strange. Litho Questa)

1988 (26 Feb). Sea Shells. T **27** and similar horiz designs. Multicoloured. W w **16** (sideways*). P 14×14½.

179	10p.	Type **27**	65	30
		w. Wmk Crown to right of CA		
180	24p.	*Margarella tropidophoroides*	1·00	60
181	29p.	*Trophon geversianus*	1·10	65
182	58p.	*Chlanidota densesculpta*	1·60	1·25
		w. Wmk Crown to right of CA	†	
179/82		Set of 4	3·75	2·50

*The normal sideways watermark shows Crown to left of CA, as seen from the back of the stamp.

(Des E. Nisbet and D. Miller (24p.), D. Miller (others). Litho Questa)

1988 (17 Sept). 300th Anniv of Lloyd's of London. Designs as T **159a** of Falkland Islands. W w **16** (sideways on 24p., 29p.). P 14.

183	10p.	brownish black and brown	40	40
184	24p.	multicoloured	75	75
185	29p.	brownish black and emerald	80	80
186	58p.	brownish black and carmine-red	1·40	1·40
183/6		Set of 4	3·00	3·00

Designs:—Vert—10p. Queen Mother at opening of new Lloyd's building, 1957; 58p. *Horatio* (tanker) on fire, 1916. Horiz—24p. *Lindblad Explorer* (cruise liner); 29p. Whaling station, Leith Harbour.

28 Glacier Headwall

29 Retracing Shackleton's Trek

48 — South Georgia & South Sandwich Islands 1989

(Des I. Loe. Litho Questa)

1989 (31 July). *Glacier Formations.* T **28** *and similar horiz designs. Multicoloured.* W w **16** *(sideways).* P 14.

187	10p. Type **28**		40	35
188	24p. Accumulation area		80	70
189	29p. Ablation area		90	80
190	58p. Calving front		1·60	1·40
187/90		Set of 4	3·25	3·00

(Des O. Bell. Litho Questa)

1989 (28 Nov). *25th Anniv of Combined Services Expedition to South Georgia.* T **29** *and similar horiz designs. Multicoloured.* W w **16** *(sideways).* P 14×14½.

191	10p. Type **29**		40	35
192	24p. Surveying at Royal Bay		90	70
193	29p. H.M.S. *Protector* (ice patrol ship)		1·00	80
194	58p. Raising Union Jack on Mount Paget		1·60	1·40
191/4		Set of 4	3·50	3·00

(Des D. Miller. Litho Questa)

1990 (15 Sept). *90th Birthday of Queen Elizabeth the Queen Mother.* Vert designs as T **165***a* (26p.) *or* **165***b* (£1) *of Falkland Islands.* W w **16**. P 14×15 (26p.) *or* 14½ (£1).

195	26p. multicoloured		1·00	1·25
196	£1 black and dull ultramarine		2·75	3·25

Designs:—26p. Queen Mother; £1 King George VI and Queen Elizabeth with A.R.P. wardens, 1940.

30 *Brutus*, Prince Olav Harbour

30a Queen Elizabeth II

(Des D. Miller. Litho Questa)

1990 (22 Dec). *Wrecks and Hulks.* T **30** *and similar vert designs. Multicoloured.* W w **16**. P 14×14½.

197	12p. Type **30**		55	40
198	26p. *Bayard*, Ocean Harbour		1·00	80
199	31p. *Karrakatta*, Husvik		1·10	95
200	62p. *Louise*, Grytviken		1·90	1·75
197/200		Set of 4	4·00	3·50

(Des D. Miller. Litho Questa)

1991 (2 July). *65th Birthday of Queen Elizabeth II and 70th Birthday of Prince Philip.* T **30***a and similar vert design. Multicoloured.* W w **16** *(sideways).* P 14½×14.

201	31p. Type **30***a*		1·00	1·40
	a. Horiz pair. Nos. 201/2 separated by label		2·00	2·75
202	31p. Prince Philip in Grenadier Guards uniform		1·00	1·40

Nos. 201/2 were printed together, se-tenant, in sheetlets of 10 (2×5) with designs alternating and the vertical rows separated by inscribed labels.

31 Contest between two Bull Elephant Seals

(Des D. Miller. Litho Questa)

1991 (2 Nov). *Elephant Seals.* T **31** *and similar horiz designs. Multicoloured.* W w **14** *(sideways).* P 14.

203	12p. Type **31**		50	50
204	26p. Adult Elephant Seal		1·00	1·00
205	29p. Seal throwing sand		1·10	1·10
206	31p. Head of Elephant Seal		1·10	1·10
207	34p. Seals on beach		1·25	1·25
208	62p. Cow seal with pup		2·00	2·00
203/8		Set of 6	6·25	6·25

(Des D. Miller. Litho Questa (68p.), Walsall (others))

1992 (6 Feb). *40th Anniv of Queen Elizabeth II's Accession. Horiz designs as* T **169***b of Falkland Islands. Multicoloured.* W w **14** *(sideways).* P 14.

209	7p. Ice-covered mountains		30	30
210	14p. Zavodovski Island		45	55
211	29p. Gulbrandsen Lake		80	95
212	34p. Three portraits of Queen Elizabeth		90	1·10
213	68p. Queen Elizabeth II		1·40	1·50
209/13		Set of 5	3·50	4·00

32 Adult Teal and Young Bird

(Des G. Drummond. Litho Questa)

1992 (12 Mar). *Endangered Species. Georgian Teal ("South Georgia Teal").* T **32** *and similar horiz designs. Multicoloured.* W w **16** *(sideways).* P 14.

214	2p. Type **32**		40	20
215	6p. Adult with eggs		50	30
216	12p. Teals swimming		70	50
217	20p. Adult and two chicks		90	90
214/17		Set of 4	2·25	1·75

(Des N. Shewring. Litho Questa)

1992 (20 June). *10th Anniv of Liberation. Square designs as* T **170***a of Falkland Islands. Multicoloured.* W w **16** *(sideways).* P 14.

218	14p. + 6p. King Edward Point		70	70
219	29p. + 11p. Queen Elizabeth 2 (liner) in Cumberland Bay		1·25	1·25
220	34p. + 16p. Royal Marines hoisting Union Jack on South Sandwich Islands		1·60	1·60
221	68p. + 32p. H.M.S. *Endurance* (ice patrol ship) and Westland AS.1 Wasp helicopter		3·00	3·00
218/21		Set of 4	6·00	6·00
MS222	116×116 mm. Nos. 218/21		6·00	6·00

The premiums on Nos. 218/22 were for the S.S.A.F.A.

33 Disused Whale Factory, Grytviken

34 Pair of Swimming Penguins

1993 South Georgia & South Sandwich Islands — 49

(Des D. Miller. Litho B.D.T.)

1993 (29 June). *Opening of South Georgia Whaling Museum.* T **33** *and similar horiz designs. Multicoloured.* W w **14** *(sideways).* P 13½.

223	15p. Type **33**		55	60
224	31p. Whaler's lighter and whale bones		1·00	1·10
225	36p. Aerial view of King Edward Cove		1·25	1·40
226	72p. Museum building		2·25	2·75
223/6		Set of 4	4·50	5·25

(Des N. Arlott. Litho Questa)

1993 (10 Dec). *Macaroni Penguin.* T **34** *and similar horiz designs. Multicoloured.* W w **14** *(sideways).* P 14½.

227	16p. Type **34**		60	45
228	34p. Group of penguins		1·25	1·00
229	39p. Two juvenile penguins		1·40	1·25
230	78p. Two adult penguins		2·25	2·50
227/30		Set of 4	5·00	4·50

35 Hourglass Dolphin

(Des R. Watton. Litho B.D.T.)

1994 (24 Jan). *Whales and Dolphins.* T **35** *and similar horiz designs. Multicoloured.* W w **14** *(sideways).* P 14.

231	1p. Type **35**		30	50
232	2p. Southern Right Whale Dolphin		40	60
233	5p. Long-finned Pilot Whale		50	70
234	8p. Southern Bottlenose Whale		65	80
235	9p. Killer Whale		70	80
236	10p. Minke Whale		70	80
237	20p. Sei Whale		1·00	1·10
238	25p. Humpback Whale		1·00	1·10
239	50p. Southern Right Whale		1·75	1·75
240	£1 Sperm Whale		2·75	3·00
241	£3 Fin Whale		6·50	7·00
242	£5 Blue Whale		10·00	11·00
231/42		Set of 12	23·00	26·00

1994 (18 Feb). *"Hong Kong '94" International Stamp Exhibition. Nos. 227/30 optd as* T **178***a of Falkland Islands.*

243	16p. Type **34**		60	75
244	34p. Group of penguins		1·25	1·50
245	39p. Two juvenile penguins		1·40	1·60
246	78p. Two adult penguins		2·25	2·50
243/6		Set of 4	5·00	5·50

36 Bull Elephant Seals

(Des D. Miller. Litho Questa)

1994 (28 Sept). *"Life in the Freezer".* T **36** *and similar multicoloured designs showing scenes from the B.B.C. Natural History Unit series.* W w **16** *(sideways on 17, 40p).* P 14½.

247	17p. Type **36**		50	75
248	35p. Young Fur Seal (*vert*)		90	1·50
249	40p. Pair of Grey-headed Albatrosses		1·60	1·75
250	65p. King Penguins in courtship display (*vert*)		2·50	2·75
247/50		Set of 4	5·00	6·00

37 Map of Jason Harbour

38 *Damien II* (research schooner)

(Des R. Watton. Litho Questa)

1994 (1 Dec). *Centenary of C.A. Larsen's First Voyage to South Georgia.* T **37** *and similar horiz designs. Multicoloured.* W w **16** *(sideways*)*.* P 14×14½.

251	17p. Type **37**		60	75
	w. Wmk Crown to right of CA		30·00	
252	35p. *Castor* (whaling ship), 1886		1·10	1·50
253	40p. *Hertha* (whaling ship), 1884		1·25	1·60
254	65p. *Jason* (whaling ship), 1881		2·25	2·75
251/4		Set of 4	4·75	6·00

*The normal sideways watermark shows Crown to left of CA, as seen from the back of the stamp.

(Des R. Watton. Litho Walsall)

1995 (8 May). *50th Anniv of End of Second World War. Multicoloured designs as* T **184***a of Falkland Islands.* W w **16** *(sideways).* P 14.

255	50p. H.M.S. *Queen of Bermuda* (armed merchant cruiser), Leith Harbour, 1941		1·75	2·00
	a. Horiz pair. Nos. 255/6		3·50	4·00
256	50p. Norwegian Defence Force 4-inch coastal gun, Hansen Point		1·75	2·00
MS257	75×85 mm. £1 Reverse of 1939–45 War Medal (*vert*). W w **14**		2·25	2·50

Nos. 255/6 were printed together, *se-tenant*, in horizontal pairs throughout the sheet, each pair forming composite design.

(Des N. Shewring. Litho Walsall)

1995 (16 Nov). *Sailing Ships.* T **38** *and similar vert designs. Multicoloured.* W w **16**. P 14½.

258	35p. Type **38**		1·25	1·75
259	40p. *Curlew* (cutter)		1·40	1·75
260	76p. *Mischief* (yacht)		2·25	2·75
258/60		Set of 3	4·50	5·50

39 Sir Ernest Shackleton and Ridge 2493

40 Chinstrap Penguin swimming

(Des M. Skidmore. Litho Walsall)

1996 (20 May). *80th Anniv of Sir Ernest Shackleton's Trek across South Georgia.* T **39** *and similar horiz designs. Multicoloured.* W w **16** *(sideways).* P 14.

261	15p. Type **39**		75	75
262	20p. Frank Worsley and King Haakon Bay		80	80
263	30p. Map of route		95	95
264	65p. Tom Crean and manager's villa, Stromness whaling station		1·40	1·40
261/4		Set of 4	3·50	3·50

50 — South Georgia & South Sandwich Islands   1996

(Des T. Chater. Litho Questa)

1996 (8 Nov). *Chinstrap Penguins. T* **40** *and similar vert designs. Multicoloured.* W w **14**. P 14½×14.
265	17p. Type **40**	55	55
266	35p. Mutual display	90	90
267	40p. Adult feeding chicks	1·10	1·10
268	76p. Feeding on krill	1·90	1·90
265/8	Set of 4	4·00	4·00

(Litho Walsall)

1997 (20 June). *Return of Hong Kong to China. Sheet* 130×90 *mm, containing design as No. 268, but with imprint date.* W w **14** *(sideways).* P 14½×14.
MS269	76p. Feeding on krill	1·75	2·00

(Des N. Shewring (No. **MS**276), D. Miller (others). Litho Questa)

1997 (10 July). *Golden Wedding of Queen Elizabeth and Prince Philip. Multicoloured designs as T* **193***a of Falkland Islands.* W w **16**. P 14½.
270	15p. Queen Elizabeth wearing red hat, 1996		50	40
	a. Horiz pair. Nos. 270/1		1·00	80
271	15p. Prince Philip in carriage-driving at Royal Windsor Horse Show		50	40
272	17p. Queen Elizabeth with show jumping team, 1993		55	45
	a. Horiz pair. Nos. 272/3		1·10	90
273	17p. Prince Philip smiling		55	45
274	40p. Princess Anne on horseback and Queen Elizabeth		1·40	1·25
	a. Horiz pair. Nos. 274/5		2·75	2·50
275	40p. Zara Phillips horse riding and Prince Philip		1·40	1·25
270/5	Set of 6		4·50	3·75
MS276	110×70 mm. £1.50, Queen Elizabeth and Prince Philip in landau *(horiz).* W w **14** *(sideways).* P 14×14½		3·50	3·75

Nos. 270/1, 272/3 and 274/5 were each printed together, se-tenant, in horizontal pairs throughout the sheets with the backgrounds forming composite designs.

41 Reindeer

42 *Explorer* (cruise ship)

(Des Sonia Felton. Litho Questa)

1998 (16 Mar). *Wildlife. Sheet,* 138×84 *mm, containing T* **41** *and similar horiz designs. Multicoloured.* W w **14** *(sideways).* P 14×13½.
MS277	35p. Type **41**; 35p. Antarctic Tern; 35p. Grey-headed Albatross; 35p. King Penguin; 35p. Prickly Burr; 35p. Fur Seal	5·00	5·00

(Des D. Miller. Litho Questa)

1998 (31 Mar). *Diana, Princess of Wales Commemoration. Sheet,* 145×70 *mm, containing vert designs as T* **196***a of Falkland Islands. Multicoloured.* W w **14** *(sideways).* P 14½×14.
MS278	35p. Laughing, 1983; 35p. In evening dress, 1996; 35p. Wearing red jacket, 1991; 35p. Wearing white jacket, 1996 *(sold at* £1.40 + 20p. *charity premium)*	3·25	3·50

(Des Kim Robertson. Litho Walsall)

1998 (28 Sept). *Tourism. T* **42** *and similar horiz designs. Multicoloured.* W w **14** *(sideways).* P 14×14½.
279	30p. Type **42**	1·10	1·00
280	35p. Wandering Albatross	1·25	1·10
281	40p. Elephant Seal	1·25	1·10
282	65p. Post Office at King Edward Point	1·75	1·75
279/82	Set of 4	4·75	4·50

43 Grytviken and Sugartop Mountain

44 H.M.S. *Resolution* in Antarctic, 1773

(Des J. Peck. Litho Walsall)

1999 (4 Jan). *Island Views. T* **43** *and similar horiz designs. Multicoloured.* W w **16** *(sideways).* P 14.
283	9p. Type **43**	45	45
284	17p. *Dias* and *Albatross* (abandoned sealing ships), Grytviken	65	65
285	30p. King Edward Point	1·10	1·10
286	40p. South Georgia from the sea	1·25	1·25
287	65p. Grytviken Church	1·50	1·50
283/7	Set of 5	4·50	4·50

(Des J. Batchelor. Litho B.D.T.)

1999 (5 Mar). *"Australia '99" World Stamp Exhibition, Melbourne. Sheet* 120×83 *mm.* W w **16**. P 13½.
MS288	**44** £1.50, multicoloured	3·25	3·25

(Des D. Miller. Litho Cartor)

1999 (18 Aug). *"Queen Elizabeth the Queen Mother's Century". Horiz designs as T* **204***a of Falkland Islands. Multicoloured (except* 30p., £1*).* W w **16** *(sideways).* P 13½.
289	25p. Visiting air-raid shelter, 1940	65	65
290	30p. With grandchildren, 1970 (black)	75	75
291	35p. With Prince William, 1994	85	85
292	40p. Presenting colour to Royal Anglian Regt	95	95
289/92	Set of 4	2·75	2·75
MS293	145×70 mm. £1 Lady Elizabeth Bowes-Lyon, 1914, and Funeral of Queen Victoria, 1901 (black)	2·75	3·00

45 Chinstrap Penguins

46 Sunrise

(Des Una Hurst. Litho Questa)

1999 (15 Nov). *Birds. T* **45** *and similar multicoloured designs.* W w **16** *(sideways on horiz designs).* P 14.
294	1p. Type **45**	10	10
295	2p. White-chinned Petrel *(horiz)*	10	10
296	5p. Grey-backed Storm Petrel	10	10
297	10p. South Georgia Pipit	20	25
298	11p. Grey-headed Albatross *(horiz)*	20	25
299	30p. Blue Petrel	60	65
300	35p. Black-browed Albatross *(horiz)*	70	75
301	40p. Georgian Diving Petrel *(horiz)*	80	85
302	50p. Macaroni Penguin	1·00	1·10
303	£1 Light-mantled Sooty Albatross *(horiz)*	2·00	2·10
304	£3 Georgian Teal ("South Georgia Pintail") *(horiz)*	6·00	6·25
305	£5 King Penguin	10·00	10·50
294/305	Set of 12	21·00	22·00

1999 South Georgia & South Sandwich Islands — 51

(Des G. Vasarhelyi. Litho Questa)

1999 (18 Dec). *New Millennium*. T **46** *and similar horiz designs. Multicoloured. W* w **16** *(sideways). P* 14½.

306	11p. Type **46**			20	25
307	11p. Grytviken Church			20	25
308	11p. Nesting Albatross			20	25
309	35p. Sunset			70	75
310	35p. Reindeer			70	75
311	35p. Penguins and chicks			70	75
306/11			Set of 6	2·50	3·00

47 Shackleton in *James Caird* crossing Scotia Sea

(Des M. Skidmore. Litho Questa)

2000 (10 Feb). *Shackleton's Trans-Antarctic Expedition, 1914–17, Commemoration.* T **47** *and similar horiz designs. Multicoloured. W* w **14** *(sideways). P* 14.

312	35p. Type **47**		70	75
313	40p. Shackleton and party approaching Stromness Whaling Station		80	85
314	65p. Shackleton's Cross at Hope Point		1·50	1·75
312/14		Set of 3	3·00	3·25

48 Prince William at Zurich Airport, 1994

(Des A. Robinson. Litho Questa)

2000 (21 June). *18th Birthday of Prince William.* T **48** *and similar multicoloured designs. W* w **14** *(sideways on 25p. and 30p.). P* 14×14½ *(vert) or* 14½×14 *(horiz)*.

315	25p. Type **48**		50	55
316	30p. Skiing in Klosters, Switzerland, 1994		60	65
317	35p. Prince William in 1997 (*horiz*)		70	75
318	40p. Prince William waving, 1999 (*horiz*)		80	85
315/18		Set of 4	2·50	2·75
MS319	175×95 mm. 50p. In Parachute Regiment uniform, 1986 (*horiz*) and Nos. 315/18. Wmk sideways. P 14½		3·50	3·75

The Ultimate Catalogue for Commonwealth Collectors

2001 BRITISH COMMONWEALTH PART 1

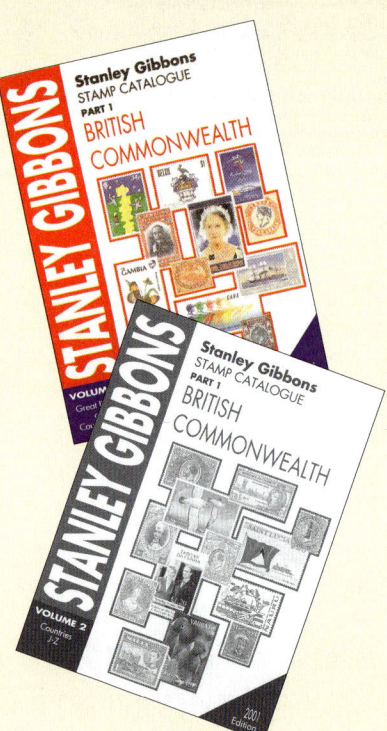

Published annually in late Autumn, Stanley Gibbons 'Part 1' is comprehensively updated and revised to include the last twelve months', new issues. This year's edition has increased and improved the listing of watermark varieties that began in previous editions. As with all Stanley Gibbons catalogues the price of each stamp has been reviewed. Therefore, it should come as no surprise that 'Part 1' is acknowledged by both stamp collectors and dealers worldwide as the industry standard for British Commonwealth stamp values.

■ 2811(01) **2001British Commonwealth Part 1 Vol. 1** (Countries A-I inc. GB) **£32.50**
■ 2812(01) **2001British Commonwealth Part 1 Vol. 2** (Countries J-Z) **£32.50**

Now Listing Even More Watermark Varities

To order or for further information, please phone our Customer Services Department for **FREE** on **0800 611 622** (UK only) quoting reference FALK/00. Alternatively, order online
www.stanleygibbons.com.

STANLEY GIBBONS

STANLEY GIBBONS PUBLICATIONS
5 Parkside, Christchurch Road, Ringwood,
Hants, BH24 3SH, United Kingdom
Tel: +44 (0)1425 472363   Fax: +44 (0)1425 470247
email: sales@stanleygibbons.co.uk

Here's Why You Should Subscribe To Britain's Leading Philatelic Magazine

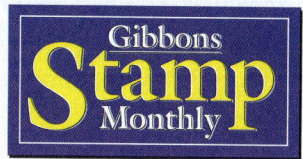

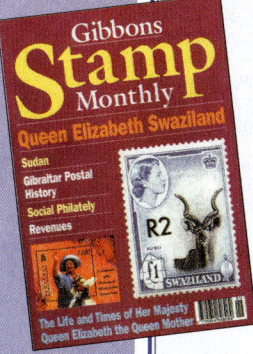

➤ Special Introductory Offer

Subscribe to GSM and you will get a Stanley Gibbons discount voucher for use against any order over £30 from our current mail order brochure.

➤ The Next 12 Issues Delivered to your Door

By taking up a subscription you're always guaranteed to receive a copy delivered direct to your door each and every month, anywhere in the world.

➤ Each Issue at the Current Cover Price

Even Britain's best value magazine has to go up in price from time to time. In the event of such increases you'll continue to receive GSM at the old cover price until it's time to renew.

➤ Free Postage & Packaging

Not only is it trouble free, but it's also post free to UK subscribers. The
subscription price you pay is no more than the cover price of the magazine.

➤ Fast & Friendly Service

You will not be dealing with an anonymous agency or a large impersonal
subscriptions sales department. All subscriptions are personally and efficiently administered from the GSM editorial office.

➤ Exclusive Subscribers Offers Every Month

GSM subscribers receive a number of unique special offers or at prices more advantageous than offered elsewhere.

**Why Should You Subscribe To GSM?
Why Shouldn't You?**

After All, How Can Thousands Of Collectors Worldwide Be Wrong!

**To Become A Subscriber To GSM Please Telephone
Pearl Parker On 01425 472363 Ext 237.
Internet: www.stanleygibbons.com**

PUT A LITTLE COLOUR IN YOUR COLLECTION

Stanley Gibbons online site gives you the opportunity to search our extensive stocks of quality stamps and related material from:

- **Great Britain**
  The widest range of Great Britain stocks available
- **Commonwealth**
  A diverse choice of quality material. Fine classics, strong provisional issues and major errors
- **Europe**
  A comprehensive range of European stock including many fine classic issues
- **The Rest of the World**
  A wide range of high quality stock from all over the world
- **Rare Items**
  Our specialist items service is backed by over 140 years of accumulated experience and knowledge
- **Country Lists**
  Search our comprehensive stock for stamps by country
- **Thematics Lists**
  Popular themes from one of the World's largest stamp stockists. Fast efficient service and despatch
- You can also view items from our extensive range of philatelic accessories, albums and award winning catalogues and online auctions.

At Stanley Gibbons the quality of our stamps is guaranteed.

www.stanleygibbons.com
Open 24 hours Everyday

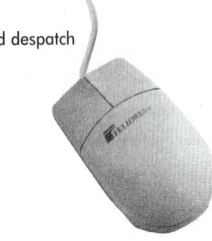